JUN 2016

P9-CMT-069

AMALFI COAST

ROAD TRIPS

This edition written and researched by

Cristian Bonetto, Duncan Garwood, Paula Hardy,
Robert Landon & Helena Smith

HOW TO USE THIS BOOK

Reviews

In the Destinations section:

All reviews are ordered in our authors' preference, starting with their most preferred option. Additionally:

Sights are arranged in the geographic order that we suggest you visit them and, within this order, by author preference.

Eating and Sleeping reviews are ordered by price range (budget, midrange, top end) and, within these ranges, by author preference.

Map Legend

Routes
- Trip Route
- Trip Detour
- Linked Trip
- Walk Route
- Tollway
- Freeway
- Primary
- Secondary
- Tertiary
- Lane
- Unsealed Road
- Plaza/Mall
- Steps
- Tunnel
- Pedestrian Overpass
- Walk Track/Path

Boundaries
- International
- State/Province
- Cliff

Hydrography
- River/Creek
- Intermittent River
- Swamp/Mangrove
- Canal
- Water
- Dry/Salt/ Intermittent Lake
- Glacier

Highway Markers
- A6 Autostrada
- SS231 State Highway
- SR203 Regional Highway
- SP3 Provincial Highway
- E74 Other Road

Trips
- 1 Trip Numbers
- 9 Trip Stop
- Walking tour
- Trip Detour

Population
- Capital (National)
- Capital (State/Province)
- City/Large Town
- Town/Village

Areas
- Beach
- Cemetery (Christian)
- Cemetery (Other)
- Park
- Forest Reservation
- Urban Area
- Sportsground

Transport
- Airport
- Cable Car/ Funicular
- Metro station
- Parking
- Train/Railway
- Tram

Symbols In This Book

- ✔ Top Tips
- 🍴 Food & Drink
- 🔗 Link Your Trips
- 🌳 Outdoors
- 💬 Tips from Locals
- 📷 Essential Photo
- ↪ Trip Detour
- 🏃 Walking Tour
- 📖 History & Culture
- 🍴 Eating
- 👪 Family
- 🛏 Sleeping

- ⊙ Sights
- 🛏 Sleeping
- ⛱ Beaches
- 🍴 Eating
- 🏃 Activities
- 🍷 Drinking
- 🎓 Courses
- ☆ Entertainment
- ☞ Tours
- 🛍 Shopping
- 🎉 Festivals & Events
- ℹ Information & Transport

These symbols and abbreviations give vital information for each listing:

- 📞 Telephone number
- ❄ Opening hours
- Ⓟ Parking
- ⊖ Nonsmoking
- ✳ Air-conditioning
- @ Internet access
- 🛜 Wi-fi access
- 🏊 Swimming pool
- 🥗 Vegetarian selection
- 📋 English-language menu
- 👶 Family-friendly

- 🐾 Pet-friendly
- 🚌 Bus
- 🚢 Ferry
- 🚋 Tram
- 🚆 Train
- apt apartments
- d double rooms
- dm dorm beds
- q quad rooms
- r rooms
- s single rooms
- ste suites
- tr triple rooms
- tw twin rooms

Note: Not all symbols displayed above appear on the maps in this book

CONTENTS

Bridge on the Amalfi Coast

WELCOME TO
THE AMALFI COAST

Naples, Pompeii and the Amalfi Coast are the Italy of your wildest dreams – a rich, intense, hypnotic ragù of Arabesque street life, decadent palaces, pastel-hued villages and aria-inspiring vistas.

With a car you'll discover there's more to Italy than Michelangelo masterpieces and Roman ruins, and you'll be able to properly explore Campania's rugged mountains, steaming fumaroles and ethereal coastal grottoes. Welcome to Italy at its most seductive and intense.

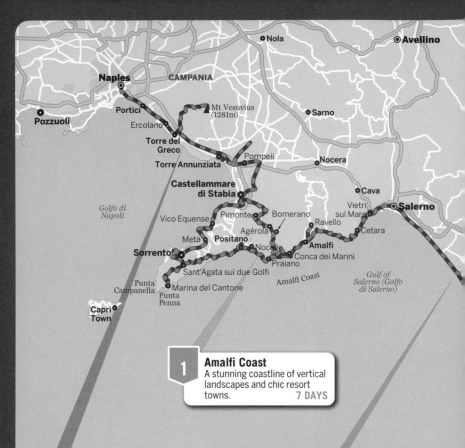

1 **Amalfi Coast**
A stunning coastline of vertical landscapes and chic resort towns. **7 DAYS**

2 **Shadow of Vesuvius**
Head from Naples' tumult to Pompeii's long-buried mysteries. **2–3 DAYS**

3 **Southern Larder**
Pair raw beauty with exuberant cuisine on Campania's coast. **3–4 DAYS**

0 — 20 km
0 — 10 miles

AMALFI COAST

★

CAMPANIA

Monti Picentini

Montecorvino

Eboli

Battipaglia

Sele

Altavilla
Silentina

Sicignano
degli Alburni

Grotte
dell'Angelo
Pertosa

BASILICATA

Paestum

Controne

Grotta di
Castelcivita

Sant'Angelo
a Fasanella

Capaccio
Scalo

Castel San
Lorenzo

Bellosguardo

Roscigno
Vecchia

Teggiano

Sala
Consilina

Padula

Agropoli

Cilento

Santa Maria di
Castellabate

Laureana
Cilento

CAMPANIA

Valle delle
Orchideo

Vallo di Diano

Castellabate

Parco Nazionale
del Cilento e
Vallo di Diano

Punta
Licosa

Sanza

Vallo della
Lucania

Pioppi

Acciaroli

Velia

Ascea

Costiera Cilentana

Pisciotta

Sapri

Golfo di
Policastro

Palinuro

Grotta
Azzurra

Camerota

San
Giovanni
a Piro

Marina di
Camerota

Grotta
Azzurra

---

4 | **Cilento Coastal Trail**
A rugged peninsula where
mountains meet the pristine
sea. **4–5 DAYS**

AMALFI COAST

HIGHLIGHTS

★

Amalfi (left) Legendary Amalfi sparkles the brightest among the glittering string of coastal gems. See it on Trips **1** **3**

Positano (above) Pearl of the Amalfi Coast, Positano is scandalously stunning, a picture-perfect composition of pastel-coloured houses tumbling down towards a deep indigo sea. See it on Trip **1**

Pompeii (right) The ruins of Pompeii are a haunting reminder of Mother Nature's merciless force and the fleeting nature of life itself. See it on Trip **2**

CITY GUIDE

NAPLES

Naples (Napoli) is an exhilarating sprawl of bombastic baroque churches, Dickensian alleyways and electrifying street life. Its in-your-face vitality can be overwhelming, but once you've found your feet you'll discover a city of regal palaces, world-renowned museums, superb pizzerias and sweeping seascapes.

Teatro San Carlo opera house (p64)

Getting Around

Neapolitan traffic is so anarchic that even Italians balk at the idea of driving here. Much of the city centre is closed to non-resident traffic, so try to leave your car as soon as you can and use public transport (bus, metro and funicular).

Parking

Street parking is not a good idea – car theft is a problem – and few hotels offer it. There's a 24-hour car park east of the city centre at Via Brin, otherwise ask your hotel for advice.

Discover the Taste of Naples

To taste authentic Neapolitan pizza, head to the *centro storico* where you'll find a number of hard-core pizzerias serving the genuine article. For a more refined meal, make for seafront Santa Lucia and the cobbled lanes of Chiaia.

Live Like a Local

For maximum atmosphere, consider the *centro storico*. Seaside Santa Lucia is home to some of the city's most prestigious hotels, and Chiaia is cool and chic. For lofty views and a chilled-out vibe, hit Vomero.

Useful Websites

I Naples (www.inaples.it) The city's official tourist-board site.

Napoli Unplugged (www.napoliunplugged.com) Attractions, up-to-date listings, articles and blog entries.

Road Trip through Naples 2

Destination coverage p54

RICHARD I'ANSON/GETTY IMAGES ©

TOP EXPERIENCES

➡ Cappella Sansevero
Marvel at human ingenuity in the Capella Sansevero, a baroque chapel where you'll find Giuseppe Sanmartino's amazing sculpture *Cristo velato* (Veiled Christ).

➡ Museo Archeologico Nazionale
Eye up classical interiors and erotica at the Museo Archeologico Nazionale, which hosts one of the world's finest collections of Graeco-Roman artefacts.

➡ Teatro San Carlo
Demand an encore at Italy's grandest opera house, which regularly stages opera, ballet and concerts.

➡ Palazzo Reale di Capodimonte
Palazzo Reale di Capodimonte might be one of Italy's less famous collections, but it's also one of its best, showcasing names such as Raphael, Titian, Caravaggio, Masaccio and El Greco.

➡ Certosa e Museo di San Martino
This charterhouse turned museum combines cloisters and carriages with romantic views.

➡ Neapolitan Street Life
There's nothing like waking up to the sound of a Neapolitan street market, whether it's rough-and-ready Porta Nolana market or the city's oldest, La Pignasecca.

Naples, Pompeii & the Amalfi Coast

For more, check out our city and country guides. lonelyplanet.com

NEED ^{TO} KNOW

CURRENCY
Euro (€)

LANGUAGE
Italian

VISAS
Generally not required for stays of up to 90 days (or at all for EU nationals); some nationalities need a Schengen visa (p128).

FUEL
You'll find filling stations on autostradas and all major roads. Reckon on approximately €1.63 for unleaded petrol and €1.35 for diesel, per litre.

RENTAL CARS
Avis (www.avis.com)

Europcar (www.europcar.com)

Hertz (www.hertz.com)

Maggiore (www.maggiore.it)

IMPORTANT NUMBERS
Ambulance (📞118)

Emergency (📞112)

Police (📞113)

Roadside Assistance
(📞803 116; 📞800 116800 from a foreign mobile phone)

Climate

Dry climate
Warm to hot summer, mild winter
Warm to hot summer, cold winter
Mild summer, cold winter
Cold climate

Rome
GO Apr–May, Jul & Nov–Dec

Naples
GO May–Jun & Sep

When to Go

High Season (Jul & Aug)
» Prices high on the coast; accommodation discounts available in some cities in August.

» Prices rocket for Christmas, New Year and Easter.

» Late December to March is high season in the Alps and Dolomites.

Shoulder Season (Apr–Jun & Sep–Oct)
» Good deals on accommodation, especially in the south.

» Spring is best for festivals, flowers and local produce.

» Autumn provides warm weather and the grape harvest.

Low Season (Nov–Mar)
» Prices at their lowest – up to 30% less than in high season.

» Many sights and hotels closed in coastal and mountainous areas.

» A good period for cultural events in large cities.

Daily Costs

Budget: Less than €100

» Double room in a budget hotel: €50–100

» Pizza or pasta: €6–12

» Excellent markets and delis for self-catering

Midrange: €100–200

» Double room in a midrange hotel: €80–180

» Lunch and dinner in local restaurants: €25–45

» Museum admission: €5–15

Top End: More than €200

» Double room in a four- or five-star hotel: €200–450

» Top-restaurant dinner: €50–150

» Opera tickets: €15–150

Eating

Restaurants (Ristoranti) Formal service and refined dishes, with prices to match.

Trattorias Family-run places with informal service and classic regional cooking.

Vegetarians Most places offer good vegetable starters and side dishes.

Price indicators for a meal with *primo* (first course), *secondo* (second course), *dolce* (dessert) and a glass of house wine:

€	less than €25
€€	€25–45
€€€	more than €45

Sleeping

Hotels From luxury boutique palaces to modest family-run *pensioni* (small hotels).

B&Bs Rooms in restored farmhouses, city *palazzi* (mansions) or seaside bungalows.

Agriturismi Farmstays range from working farms to luxury rural retreats.

Price indicators for a double room with bathroom:

€	less than €100
€€	€100–200
€€€	more than €200

Arriving in Italy

Capodichino Airport (Naples)

Rental cars Agencies are located in the main Arrivals hall.

Airport shuttles Run every 20 minutes from 6.30am to 11.40pm.

Taxis Set fare €19 to €23; 30 minutes.

Leonardo da Vinci (Fiumicino) Airport (Rome)

Rental cars Agencies are near the multilevel car park. Look for signs in the Arrivals area.

Trains & buses Run every 30 minutes from 6.30am to 11.40pm.

Night buses Hourly departures from 12.30am to 5am.

Taxis Set fare €48; 45 minutes.

Malpensa Airport (Milan)

Rental cars In Terminal 1 agencies are on the 1st floor; in Terminal 2 in the Arrivals hall.

Malpensa Express & Shuttle Runs every 30 minutes from 5am to 11pm.

Night buses Limited services from 12.15am to 5am.

Taxis Set fare €90; 50 minutes.

Mobile Phones (Cell Phones)

Local SIM cards can be used in European, Australian and unlocked, multiband US phones. Other phones must be set to roaming.

Internet Access

Wi-fi is available in many lodgings and city bars, often free. Internet cafes are thin on the ground and typically charge €2 to €6 per hour.

Money

ATMs at airports, most train stations and in towns and cities. Credit cards accepted in most hotels and restaurants. Keep cash for immediate expenses.

Tipping

Not obligatory but round up the bill in pizzerias and trattorias; 10% is normal in upmarket restaurants.

Useful Websites

Italia (www.italia.it) Official tourism site.

Michelin (www.viamichelin.it) A useful route planner.

Agriturismi (www.agriturismi.it) Guide to farmstays.

Lonely Planet (www.lonelyplanet.com/italy) Destination lowdown.

For more, see Road Trip Essentials (p114).

Road Trips

Sorrento (p72)
ELLEN VAN BODEGOM/GETTY IMAGES ©

Amalfi Coast

1

Not for the fainthearted, this trip along the Amalfi Coast tests your driving skill on a 108km stretch, featuring dizzying hairpin turns and pastel-coloured towns draped over sea-cliff scenery.

TRIP HIGHLIGHTS

25 km

Sant'Agata sui due Golfi
The region's most panoramic views

83 km

Ravello
Ravishing gardens and stupendous coastal views

FINISH
Vietri sul Mare

Vico Equense

START

Sorrento

3

5

8

9

Praiano

76 km

Amalfi
Sun-filled piazzas overlook a gorgeous stretch of beach

Marina del Cantone

Positano
The coast's swankiest and most photogenic town

60 km

7 DAYS
108KM / 67 MILES

GREAT FOR...

BEST TIME TO GO
Summer for best beach weather, but also peak crowds.

ESSENTIAL PHOTO
Positano's vertiginous stack of pastel-coloured houses cascading down to the sea.

BEST FOR OUTDOORS
Hiking Ravello and its environs.

Left Villa Rufolo, Ravello (p23)

1 Amalfi Coast

The Amalfi Coast is about drama, and this trip takes you where mountains plunge seaward in a stunning vertical landscape of precipitous crags, forests and resort towns. Positano and Amalfi are fabulously picturesque and colourful, while mountain-top Ravello is a serenely tranquil place with a tangible sense of history. Cars are useful for inland exploration, as are your own two legs. Walking trails provide a wonderful escape from the coastal clamour.

❶ Vico Equense (p83)

The Bay of Naples is justifiably famous for its pizza, which was invented here as a savoury way to highlight two local specialities: mozzarella and sun-kissed tomatoes. Besides its pretty little *centro storico* (historic centre), this little clifftop town overlooking the Bay of Naples boasts some of the region's best pizza, including a by-the-metre version at **Ristorante & Pizzeria da Gigino**

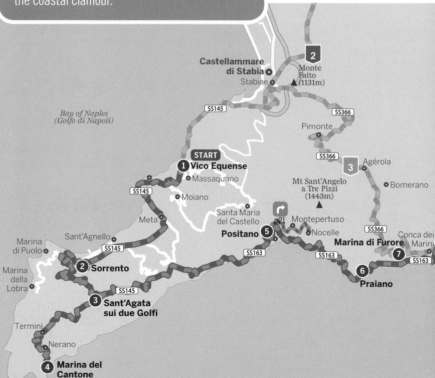

(☎081 879 83 09; www.pizza metro.it; Via Nicotera 15; pizza per metre €12-26; ⊗noon-1am; ⚑).

The Drive » From Vico Equense to Sorrento, your main route will be the SS145 roadway for 12km. Expect to hug the sparkling coastline after Marina di Equa before venturing inland around Meta.

- - - - - - - - - - - - - -

② Sorrento (p72)

On paper, cliff-straddling Sorrento is a place to avoid – a package-holiday centre with few sights, no beach to speak of and a glut of brassy English-style pubs. In reality,

it's strangely appealing, its laid-back southern Italian charm resisting all attempts to swamp it in souvenir tat and graceless development.

According to Greek legend, it was in Sorrento's waters that the mythical sirens once lived. Sailors of antiquity were powerless to resist the beautiful song of these charming maidens-cum-monsters, who would lure them to their doom.

The Drive » Take the SS145 (Via Nastro Azzurro) for 11km to Sant'Agata sui due Golfi. Sun-

dappled village streets give way to forest as you head further inland.

TRIP HIGHLIGHT

③ Sant'Agata sui due Golfi (p81)

Perched high in the hills above Sorrento, sleepy Sant'Agata sui due Golfi commands spectacular views of the Bay of Naples on one side and the Bay of Salerno on the other (hence its name, Saint Agatha on the two Gulfs). The best viewpoint is the **Deserto** (☎081 878 01 99; Via Deserto; ⊗gardens 8am-7pm, lookout 10am-noon & 5-7pm summer, 10am-noon & 3-5pm winter), a Carmelite convent 1.5km uphill from the village centre.

The Drive » From Sant'Agata sui due Golfi to Marina del Cantone it's a 9km drive, the last part involving some serious hairpin turns. Don't let the gorgeous sea views distract you.

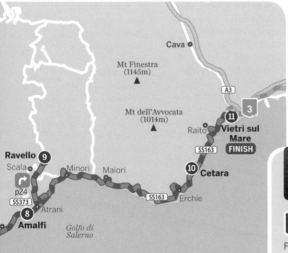

Cava

Mt Finestra (1145m) ▲

A3

Mt dell'Avvocata (1014m) ▲

Raito ⑪ **Vietri sul Mare**

SS163 **FINISH**

③

Ravello ⑨

Scala

Minori Maiori

p24

SS373

⑧

Amalfi Atrani

Golfo di Salerno

SS163 Erchie

⑩ **Cetara**

⊙ 0 ——— 5 km
Ⓝ 0 ——— 2.5 miles

LINK YOUR TRIP

2 Shadow of Vesuvius

Follow the curve of the Bay of Naples, from simmering Vesuvius to roiling Naples (p27).

3 Southern Larder

From Sorrento to Paestum, this trip takes you to the heart of mozzarella country (p37).

❹ Marina del Cantone (p82)

From Nerano, where you'll park, a beautiful hiking trail leads down to the stunning Bay of Ieranto and one of the coast's top swimming spots, Marina del Cantone. This unassuming village with its small pebble beach is a lovely, tranquil place to stay as well as a popular diving destination. The village also has a reputation as a gastronomic hot spot and VIPs regularly catch a boat over from Capri to dine here.

The Drive » First, head back up that switchback to Sant'Agata sui due Golfi. Catch the SS145 and then the SS163 as they weave their way along bluffs and cliffsides to Positano. Most of the 24km involve stunning sea views.

TRIP HIGHLIGHT

❺ Positano (p85)

The pearl in the pack, Positano is the coast's most photogenic and expensive town. Its steeply stacked houses are a medley of peaches, pinks and terracottas, and its near-vertical streets (many of which are, in fact, staircases) are lined with voguish shop displays, elegant hotels and smart restaurants. Look closely, though, and you'll find reassuring signs of everyday reality – crumbling stucco, streaked paintwork and occasionally a faint whiff of problematic drainage.

John Steinbeck visited in 1953 and wrote in an article for *Harper's Bazaar*: 'Positano bites deep. It is a dream place that isn't quite real when you are there and becomes beckoningly real after you have gone.'

The Drive » From Positano to Praiano it's a quick 8km spin on the SS163, passing Il San Pietro di Positano at the halfway point, then heading southeast along the peninsula's edge.

❻ Praiano (p91)

An ancient fishing village, a low-key summer resort and, increasingly, a popular centre for the arts, Praiano is a delight. With no centre as such, its whitewashed houses pepper the verdant ridge of Monte Sant'Angelo as it slopes towards Capo Sottile. Formerly an important silk-production centre, it was a favourite of the Amalfi doges (dukes), who made it their summer residence.

For those willing to take the plunge, the **Centro Sub Costiera Amalfitana** (☎089 81 21 48; www.centrosub.it; Via Marina di Praia; ▲) runs beginner to expert dives (€80 to €130) exploring the area's coral, marine life and grottoes.

The Drive » From Praiano, Marina di Furore is just 3km further on, past beautiful coves that cut into the shoreline.

❼ Marina di Furore (p92)

A few kilometres further on, Marina di Furore sits at the bottom of what's known as the fjord of Furore, a giant cleft that cuts through the Lattari

THE BLUE RIBBON DRIVE

Stretching from Vietri sul Mare to Sant'Agata sui due Golfi near Sorrento, the SS163, nicknamed the Nastro Azzurro (Blue Ribbon), remains one of Italy's most stunning roadways. Commissioned by Bourbon king Ferdinand II and completed in 1853, it wends its way along the Amalfi Coast's entire length, snaking round impossibly tight curves, over deep ravines and through tunnels gouged out of sheer rock. It's a magnificent feat of civil engineering although, as John Steinbeck pointed out in a 1953 essay, the road is also 'carefully designed to be a little narrower than two cars side by side'.

mountains. The main village, however, stands 300m above, in the upper Vallone del Furore. A one-horse place that sees few tourists, it breathes a distinctly rural air despite the presence of colourful murals and unlikely modern sculpture.

The Drive » From Marina di Furore to Amalfi, the sparkling Mediterranean Sea will be your escort as you drive westward along the SS163 coastal road for 6km. Look for Vettica Minore and Conca dei Marini along the way, along with fluffy bunches of fragrant cypress trees.

TRIP HIGHLIGHT

8 Amalfi (p92)

It is hard to grasp that pretty little Amalfi, with its sun-filled piazzas and small beach, was once a maritime superpower with a population of more than 70,000. For one thing, it's not a big place – you can easily walk from one end to the other in about 20 minutes. For another, there are very few historical buildings of note. The explanation is chilling – most of the old city, along with its populace, simply slid into the sea during an earthquake in 1343.

One happy exception is the striking **Cattedrale di Sant'Andrea** (Piazza del Duomo; ⏱7.30am-7.45pm), parts of which date from the early 10th century. Although the

WALK OF THE GODS

Probably the best-known walk on the Amalfi Coast, the 12km, six-hour **Sentiero degli Dei** (Walk of the Gods) follows the steep paths linking Positano to Praiano. The walk commences at **Via Chiesa Nuova**, just north of the SS163 road, in the northern part of Positano. Not advised for vertigo sufferers, it's a spectacular, meandering trail along the pinnacle of the mountains where caves and terraces plummet dramatically from the cliffs to deep valleys framed by the brilliant blue of the sea. It can sometimes be foggy in the dizzy heights, but that somehow adds to the drama, with the cypresses rising through the mist like dark shimmering sword blades.

building is a hybrid, the Sicilian Arabic-Norman style predominates, particularly in the two-tone masonry and the 13th-century bell tower.

Be sure to take the short walk around the headland to neighbouring Atrani, a picturesque tangle of whitewashed alleys and arches centred on a lively, lived-in piazza and popular beach.

DETOUR: NOCELLE

Start: 5 Positano

A tiny, still relatively isolated mountain village above Positano, Nocelle (450m) commands some of the most spectacular views on the entire coast. A world apart from touristy Positano, it's a sleepy, silent place where not much ever happens, nor would its few residents ever want it to.

If you want to stay, consider delightful **Villa della Quercia** (☎089 812 34 97; www.villadellaquercia.com; r €70-80; 🖥), a former monastery with spectacular views. For food, **Trattoria Santa Croce** (www.ristorantesantacrocepositano.com; Via Nocelle 19; ⏱noon-2.30pm & 7-11pm Apr-Oct) is a reliable low-key restaurant in the main part of the village.

Nocelle lies eight very windy kilometres northeast of Positano. Hikers tackling the Sentiero degli Dei might want to stop off as they pass through.

WHY THIS IS A CLASSIC TRIP
ROBERT LANDON, AUTHOR

Since the time of the Caesars, the Amalfi Coast has represented the ultimate luxury getaway. It only makes sense, since this coastline – an absurdly beautiful conjunction of craggy cliffs, lush forests, near-vertical townscapes and azure seas – forces you to forget life's daily woes. And when you're ready, you can quickly escape the clamouring coast on some of Italy's most jaw-dropping hikes.

Top: Highway motorcycling on the Amalfi Coast
Left: Cliffside road, Atrani (p21)
Right: Positano (p20)

The Drive » Start the 9km trip from Amalfi to Ravello by heading along the coast and then catching the SS373 near Castiglione. Breathtaking views abound on this narrow coastal road, before you head up to hillside Ravello.

- - - - - - - - -

TRIP HIGHLIGHT

9 Ravello (p98)

Sitting high in the hills above Amalfi, refined Ravello is a polished town almost entirely dedicated to tourism. Boasting impeccable bohemian credentials – Richard Wagner, DH Lawrence and Virginia Woolf all lounged here – it's known today for its ravishing gardens and stupendous views, the best in the world according to former resident Gore Vidal.

To enjoy these views, head south of Ravello's cathedral to the 14th-century tower that marks the entrance to **Villa Rufolo** (☏080 85 76 21; adult/reduced €5/3; ⏰9am-5pm). Created by Scotsman Scott Neville Reid in 1853, these gardens combine celestial panoramic views, exotic colours, artistically crumbling towers and luxurious blooms. Also worth seeking out is the wonderful **Camo** (☏089 85 74 61; Piazza Duomo 9; ⏰9.30am-noon & 3-5.30pm Mon-Sat). Squeezed between tourist-driven shops, this very special place is, on the face of it, a cameo shop. And

23

DETOUR: RAVELLO WALKS

Start: 9 Ravello

Ravello is the starting point for numerous walks that follow ancient paths through the surrounding Lattari mountains. If you've got the legs for it, you can walk down to **Minori** via an attractive route of steps, hidden alleys and olive groves, passing the picturesque hamlet of **Torello** en route. This walk kicks off just to the left of Villa Rufolo and takes around 45 minutes. Alternatively, you can head the other way, to Amalfi, via the ancient village of **Scala**. Once a flourishing religious centre with more than a hundred churches and the oldest settlement on the Amalfi Coast, Scala is now a pocket-sized sleepy place where the wind whistles through empty streets, and gnarled locals go patiently about their daily chores. In the central square, the Romanesque **duomo** (Piazza Municipio; ⏰ 8am-noon & 5-7pm) retains some of its 12th-century solemnity. Ask at the Ravello tourist office for more information on local walks.

exquisite they are too, crafted primarily out of coral and shell. But don't stop here; ask to see the treasure trove of a museum beyond the showroom.

The Drive » Head back down to the SS163 for a 19km journey that twists and turns challengingly along the coast to Cetara. Pine trees and a variety of flowering shrubs line the way.

- - - - - - - - - - - - - -

⑩ Cetara (p103)

Cetara is a picturesque, tumbledown fishing village with a reputation as a gastronomic delight. Since medieval times it has been an important fishing centre, and today its deep-sea tuna fleet is considered one of the Mediterranean's most important. At night, fishermen set out in small boats armed with powerful lamps to fish for anchovies. No surprise then that tuna and anchovies dominate local menus, especially at Al Convento (p103), a sterling seafood restaurant near the small harbour.

The Drive » From Cetara to Vietri sul Mare, head northeast for 6km on the SS163 for more twisting, turning and stupendous views across the Golfo di Salerno.

- - - - - - - - - - - - - -

⑪ Vietri sul Mare (p103)

Marking the end of the coastal road, Vietri sul Mare is the ceramics capital of Campania. Although production dates back to Roman times, it didn't take off as an industry until the 16th and 17th centuries. Today, ceramics shopaholics find their paradise at the **Ceramica Artistica Solimene** (📞089 21 02 43; www.ceramicasolimene. it; Via Madonna degli Angeli 7; ⏰9am-7pm Mon-Fri, 10am-1pm & 4-7pm Sat), a vast factory outlet. Devotees should also seek out the **Museo della Ceramica** (Museum of Ceramics; 📞089 21 18 35; Villa Guerriglia; ⏰9am-3pm Tue-Sat, 9.30am-1pm Sun) in the nearby village of Raito. Housed in a lovely villa surrounded by a park, the museum has a comprehensive collection.

Right Italian cuisine, Cetara

Shadow of Vesuvius

2

Beginning in the tumult that is Naples, this trip winds around the Bay of Naples to the ruins of Pompeii and Herculaneum to seaside Sorrento – even daring the slopes of Vesuvius itself.

TRIP HIGHLIGHTS

0 km

Naples
Incomparable city of bombastic baroque and electrifying street life

20 km

Mt Vesuvius
The crater offers views into the lofty menace

1 START

5

10 km

Herculaneum
Superbly preserved ruins, from ancient advertisements to skeleton remains of the terror-struck

3

Oplontis

8

55 km

Pompeii
These celebrated ruins still conjure visions of Vesuvius

Castellammare di Stabia

Sorrento
FINISH

2–3 DAYS
90KM / 56 MILES

GREAT FOR...

BEST TIME TO GO
Spring and autumn for best weather, December for stunning Christmas displays.

ESSENTIAL PHOTO
Capture Vesuvius' brooding majesty from Naples' waterfront.

BEST FOR HISTORY
Relive history amid Herculaneum's ruins.

Shadow of Vesuvius

This trip begins in Naples (Napoli), a city that rumbles with contradictions — grimy streets hit palm-fringed boulevards; crumbling facades mask golden baroque ballrooms. You quickly reach some of the world's most spectacular Roman ruins including Pompeii and Herculaneum, as well as lesser-known jewels, from salubrious ancient villas to Portici's royal getaway. Above it all looms Vesuvius' dark beauty.

TRIP HIGHLIGHT

❶ Naples (p54)

Italy's most misunderstood city is also one of its finest – an exhilarating mess of baroque churches, bellowing baristas and electrifying street life. Contradiction is the catchphrase here. It's a place where anarchy, pollution and crime sidle up to lavish palaces, mighty museums and aristocratic tailors.

The Unesco-listed *centro storico* (historic city centre) is an

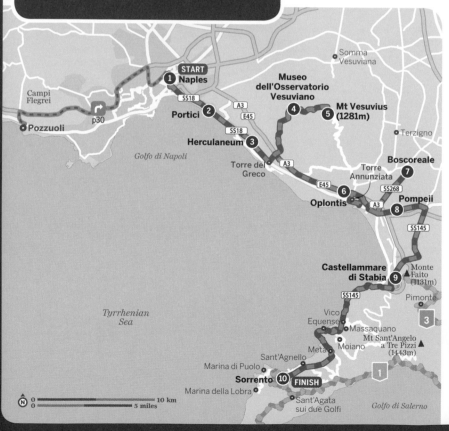

intoxicating warren of streets packed with ancient churches, citrus-filled cloisters and first-rate pizzerias. It's here, under the washing lines, that you'll find classic Neapolitan street life – overloaded Vespas hurtling through cobbled alleyways and clued-up *casalinghe* (homemakers) bullying market vendors. Move towards the sea and the cityscape opens up. Imperious palaces flank show-off squares where Gucci-clad shoppers strut their stuff, then lunch in chandeliered cafes. This is Royal Naples, the Naples of the Bourbons that so impressed the 18th-century grand tourists.

LINK YOUR TRIP

1 Amalfi Coast
Sorrento kicks off this week-long adventure of hairpin turns and vertical landscapes amid the world's most glamorous stretch of coastline (p17).

3 Southern Larder
From Sorrento, you can embark on this culinary adventure along the Amalfi Coast and the Golfo di Salerno, where mozzarella rules the roost (p37).

To buff up for Pompeii and Herculaneum, head to the **Museo Archeologico Nazionale** (☎081 442 21 49; Piazza Museo Nazionale 19; adult/reduced €8/4; ⏲9am-7.30pm Wed-Mon). With one of the world's finest collections of Graeco-Roman artefacts, it stars a small but stunning collection of mosaics, mostly from Pompeii, plus a room full of ancient erotica.

The Drive ⟩⟩ A straight 8km drive along the SS18 provides an easy journey from central Naples straight to the Palazzo Reale di Portici – if the other drivers behave, of course.

❷ Portici

The town of Portici lies at the foot of Mt Vesuvius and had to be rebuilt in the wake of its ruin by the 1631 eruption. Charles III of Spain, king of Naples and Sicily, erected his stately royal **palace** (Via Università 101; ⏲irregular) here between 1738 and 1748. After the fall of the Bourbons and Italy's unification in 1860, the palace found new life as the Portici botanic gardens and the Royal Higher School of Agriculture. Today, the exquisite botanic gardens are operated by the University of Naples Federico II.

The Drive ⟩⟩ The entrance to the ruins of Herculaneum lies just down the street, a few hundred metres down the SS18.

TRIP HIGHLIGHT

❸ Herculaneum (p65)

Superbly conserved, the ruins of ancient **Herculaneum** (☎081 732 43 27; www.pompeiisites.org; Corso Resina 187, Ercolano; adult/reduced €11/5.50, incl Pompeii €20/10; ⏲8.30am-7.30pm summer, to 5pm winter) are smaller, less daunting and easier to navigate than Pompeii. They also include some of the area's richest archaeological finds, from ancient advertisements and mosaics to carbonised furniture and skeletons of people who died cowering in terror.

Destroyed by an earthquake in AD 63, Herculaneum was completely submerged in the AD 79 eruption of Mt Vesuvius. However, because it was much closer to the volcano than Pompeii, it drowned in a sea of mud, essentially fossilising the town and ensuring that even delicate items were discovered remarkably well preserved.

Look out for the **Casa d'Argo**, a well-preserved example of a Roman noble family's house, complete with porticoed garden and *triclinium* (dining area). **Casa dei Cervi** (House of the Deer) is an imposing example of a Roman nobleman's villa, with two stories ranged around a central courtyard and animated with murals and still-life paintings. And don't miss the 1st-century-AD **Terme Suburbane** (Suburban Baths; closed for restoration at writing), with deep pools, stucco friezes and bas-reliefs looking down upon marble seats and floors.

The Drive » The museum is only 10km from Herculaneum. Keep heading down the SS18 until you reach the centre of Torre del Greco, where you will turn right on Via Vittorio Veneto, which will quickly turn into Via Guglielmo Marconi. Follow the signs as you wind your way

up the lower elevations of Mt Vesuvius, and the Bay of Naples comes into view.

---

❹ Museo dell'Osservatorio Vesuviano

Halfway up Mt Vesuvius, this **museum** (Museum of the Vesuvian Observatory; (☏081 610 84 83; www.ov.ingv.it; Via dell'Osservatorio 14, Ercolano; admission free; ☺9am-4pm Mon-Fri, 10am-4pm Sat & Sun Apr-Jul, 9am-2pm Mon-Fri, 10am-2pm Sat & Sun Sep-Mar) contains an interesting array of artefacts telling the history of 2000 years

DETOUR: CAMPI FLEGREI

Start: ❶ Naples

Stretching west of Posillipo Hill to the Tyrrhenian Sea, the oft-overlooked Campi Flegrei (Phlegrean Fields) counterbalances its ugly urban sprawl with steamy active craters, lush volcanic hillsides and priceless ancient ruins. While its Greek settlements are Italy's oldest, its Monte Nuovo is Europe's youngest mountain. It's not every week that a mountain just appears on the scene. At 8pm on 29 September 1538, a crack appeared in the earth near the ancient Roman settlement of Tripergole, spewing out a violent concoction of pumice, fire and smoke over six days. By the end of the week, Pozzuoli had a new 134m-tall neighbour.

Today, Europe's newest mountain is a lush and peaceful nature reserve. Before exploring the Campi Flegrei, stop at the helpful **tourist office** (☏081 526 14 81; www.infocampiflegrei.it; Largo Matteotti 1a; ☺9am-3pm Mon-Fri) in Pozzuoli to pick up tourist information and maps of the area, and purchase a €4 cumulative ticket that covers most of the key archaeological sites.

of Vesuvius-watching. Founded in 1841 to monitor Vesuvius' moods, it is the oldest volcanic observatory in the world. To this day, scientists are still constantly monitoring the active volcanoes at Vesuvius, Campi Flegrei and Ischia.

The Drive » It's many more hairpin turns as you make your way along the same road almost to Vesuvius' crater, about 7km away. Views across the Bay of Naples and Campania are magnificent.

TRIP HIGHLIGHT

❺ Mt Vesuvius (p66)

Since exploding into history in AD 79, Vesuvius has blown its top more than 30 times. The most devastating of these was in 1631, and the most recent was in 1944. It is the only volcano on the European mainland to have erupted within the last hundred years. What redeems this lofty menace is the spectacular view from its **crater** (☏081 239 56 53; adult/reduced €10/8; ☺9am-6pm Jul & Aug, to 5pm Apr-Jun & Sep, to 4pm Mar & Oct, to 3pm Nov-Feb, ticket office closes 1hr before the crater) – a breathtaking panorama that takes in sprawling city, sparkling islands, and the Monti Picentini, part of the Apennine mountains.

The end of the road is the summit car park and the ticket office.

From here, a relatively easy 860m path leads up to the summit (allow 35 minutes), best tackled in sneakers and with a jacket in tow (it can be chilly up top, even in summer). When the weather is bad the summit path is shut and bus departures are suspended.

The Drive » The first part of this 21km stretch heads back down Vesuvius the same way you came up. Head all the way down to the A3 highway, turn left onto it and head southeast. The villas of Oplontis are just off the Torre Annunziata exit.

Mosaics from Pompeii, Museo Archeologico Nazionale, Naples (p55)

6 Oplontis (p67)

Buried beneath the unappealing streets of modern-day Torre Annunziata, Oplontis was once a seafront suburb under the administrative control of Pompeii. First discovered in the 18th century, only two of its houses have been unearthed, and only one, **Villa Poppaea** (www.pompeiisites.org; Via dei Sepolcri, Torre Annunziata; admission €5.50; ⏰8.30am-5pm), is open to the public. This villa is a magnificent example of an *otium* villa (a residential building used for rest and recreation), and may once have belonged to Emperor Nero's second wife.

The Drive » This brief 5km jaunt has you once again heading south on the SS18 to SS268 (Via Settetermini), which leads through scruffy Neapolitan suburbs to the Antiquarium di Boscoreale.

7 Boscoreale (p67)

Inaugurated in 1991, the **Antiquarium di Boscoreale** (www.pompeiisites.org; Via Settetermini 15, admission €5.50; ⏰8.30am-5pm, to 6pm Apr-Oct) is a modern museum dedicated to life before the AD 79 eruption. Located on the lower slopes of Vesuvius, it holds a treasure trove of artefacts from Pompeii, Herculaneum and the surrounding region.

The Drive » Head straight back down the SS268 for about 4km all the way back to the SS18, which will take you through about 2km of scruffy suburbs right up next to the ruins of Pompeii.

VESUVIAN WINES

Vesuvian wine has been relished since ancient times. The rare combination of rich volcanic soil and a favourable microclimate created by its slopes make the territory one of Italy's most interesting viticultural areas. Lacryma Christi (literally 'tears of Christ') is the name of perhaps the most celebrated wine produced on the slopes of Mt Vesuvius. Other prized vintages include Piedirosso, Aglianico and Greco del Vesuvio.

WHY THIS IS A CLASSIC TRIP
ROBERT LANDON,
AUTHOR

After two millennia, the explosion of Mt Vesuvius is still fresh in our collective imaginations. On this trip you not only wander among the ruins of Roman cities frozen in time by the eruption, but actually glimpse into the infamous crater itself. And of course the trip kicks off in the sublime madness of Naples, an unruly and beautiful city unlike any other in Italy.

Top: Vico Equense (p83) with Mt Vesuvius in the distance
Left: Hikers ascend Mt Vesuvius
Right: Pompeii archeological site

TRIP HIGHLIGHT

8 Pompeii (p66)

Nothing piques human curiosity like a mass catastrophe, and few beat the ruins of **Pompeii** (📞081 857 53 47; www. pompeiisites.org; entrances at Porta Marina, Piazza Esedra & Piazza Anfiteatro; adult/reduced €11/5.50, incl Herculaneum €20/10; ⏱8.30am-7.30pm summer, to 5pm winter), a stark reminder of Vesuvius' malign forces.

Of Pompeii's original 66 hectares, 44 have now been excavated. However, expect a noticeable lack of clear signage, areas cordoned off for no apparent reason, and the odd stray dog. Audio guides (€6.50) are a sensible investment, and a good guidebook will help – try the €10 *Pompeii* published by Electa Napoli. To do justice to the site, allow at least three hours.

Highlights include the site's main entrance at **Porta Marina**, the most impressive of the seven gates that punctuated the ancient town walls. Just outside the wall is the impressive **Terme Suburbane**. These baths are famed for the risqué frescoes in the *apodyterium* (changing room). Immediately on the right as you enter Porta Marina is the 1st-century-BC **Tempio**

TOP TIP: PASS TO THE PAST

You can visit all five key sites around Pompeii, including the ruins of Pompeii and Herculaneum as well as the Antiquarium di Boscoreale, Oplontis and Stabiae, with a single pass that costs €20 and is valid for three days. It is available at the ticket offices of all five sites.

di Venere (Temple of Venus), formerly one of the town's most opulent temples. The **Tempio di Apollo** (Temple of Apollo) is the oldest and most important of Pompeii's religious buildings, dating to the 2nd century BC. And the **Villa dei Misteri**, one of the most complete structures left standing in Pompeii, contains the remarkable fresco *Dionysiac Frieze*. One of the world's largest ancient paintings, it depicts the initiation of a bride-to-be into the cult of Dionysus, the Greek god of wine.

The Drive » The 9km trip from Pompeii begins heading south along the SS145 (Corso Italia). It will take you through a mixture of suburbs and small farms. Ahead, you will see the mountains of the Amalfi Coast rear up. The ancient villas of Stabiae are just east of Corso Italia, off Via Giuseppe Cosenza.

---

⑨ Castellammare di Stabia (p67)

South of Oplontis in modern-day Castellammare di Stabia, Stabiae was once a popular resort for wealthy Romans. It stood on the slopes of the Varano hill overlooking the entire Bay of Naples, and according to ancient historian Pliny it was lined for miles with extravagant villas. You can visit two **villas** (www.pompeiisites.org; Via Passeggiata Archeologica; admission €5.50; ⊙8.30am-6pm): the 1st-century-BC Villa Arianna and the larger Villa San Marco, said to measure more than 11,000 sq metres.

The Drive » This trip is a bit longer, at 21km, than the last few. Head back to the SS145, which will soon head over to the coast. Enjoy beautiful views over the Bay of Naples as you wind your way past Vico Equense, Meta and Piano di Sorrento to Sorrento.

---

⑩ Sorrento (p72)

For an unabashed tourist town, Sorrento still manages to preserve the feeling of a civilised coastal retreat. Even the souvenirs are a cut above the norm, with plenty of fine old shops selling ceramics, lacework and marquetry items. It is also the spiritual home of *limoncello*, a delicious lemon liqueur traditionally made from the zest of Femminello St Teresa lemons, also known as Sorrento lemons. Its tart sweetness makes the perfect nightcap, as well as a brilliant flavouring for both sweet and savoury dishes.

Right Shopping on the streets of Sorrento

Southern Larder **3**

From the Amalfi Coast to Paestum, this trip packs in both jaw-dropping natural beauty and mouth-watering cuisine built on fresh fish, sun-kissed veggies and the world's finest mozzarella.

TRIP HIGHLIGHTS

0 km

Sorrento
Civilised coastal resort and spiritual home of *limoncello* liqueur

83 km

Paestum
Indulge in great Greek ruins and the world's best mozzarella

Cetara

Vico Equense

START ①

⑥ ⑦

⑩
FINISH

35 km

Conca dei Marini
Seaside birthplace of the scrumptious *sfogliatella* pastry

39 km

Amalfi
A medieval naval power famous for its *scialatielli* pasta

3–4 DAYS
83KM / 52 MILES

GREAT FOR...

BEST TIME TO GO
Spring for sunny, clear weather; early autumn for abundant produce.

ESSENTIAL PHOTO
Capture the hypnotically terraced cliffs of Agerola at sunset.

BEST FOR FOODIES
Going to mozzarella's source in Paestum.

Left House decorated with pumpkins, Sorrento (p38)

3 Southern Larder

Besides the raw natural beauty of the Amalfi Coast and Gulf of Sorrento, this trip is a gourmand's dream. Foodies flock here from the world over for local specialities such as *limoncello* (lemon liqueur), ricotta-stuffed *sfogliatella* pastries, and a wildly creamy concoction made from water-buffalo milk that gives the word 'mozzarella' a whole new meaning. Burn off the extra calories hiking the Amalfi's jaw-dropping coastal trails or clambering over Paestum's majestic Greek ruins.

TRIP HIGHLIGHT

1 Sorrento (p72)
Most people come to seaside Sorrento as a pleasant stopover between Capri, Naples and the Amalfi Coast. It boasts dramatic views of the Bay of Naples and a festive holiday feel. However, foodies converge here for a very specific treat: *limoncello*, a very simple lemon liqueur made from the zest of lemons (preferably the local Femminello St Teresa lemons), plus

sugar and grain alcohol. It is traditionally served after dinner in chilled ceramic cups, and its combination of sweetness and biting tartness make the perfect end to a meal.

The Drive » Head north on the SS145, including a beautiful stretch along the Bay of Naples, for 12km to Vico Equense.

---

② Vico Equense (p83)

Known to the Romans as Aequa, Vico Equense is a small cliff-top town east of Sorrento. Largely bypassed by international tourists, it's a laid-back, authentic place worth a quick stopover, if only to experience some of the famous pizza served by the metre at the justly celebrated **Ristorante & Pizzeria da Gigino** ([☎]081 879 83 09; www.pizzametro. it; Via Nicotera 15; pizza per metre €12-26; ⊙noon-1am; [👫]). This is no tourist trap but a beloved local institution due to its fresh ingredients and fluffy dough.

The Drive » From Vico Equense to Pimonte is 18km. You'll again hug the beautiful Bay of Naples for a while, reaching the turn-off for the SS366 in Castellammare di Stabia. From here, head inland and uphill as you wind your way to Pimonte.

---

③ Pimonte

Tucked into the mountains in the easternmost end of the Amalfi peninsula, this small rural town is a far cry from the high-rolling coast, with tractors trundling through the narrow streets. Make a point of stopping at the main piazza for the delicious almond-based speciality *torta palummo* at Caffè Palumma. Expect curious stares; tourists are a rarity here.

The Drive » The 8km drive from Pimonte to Agerola takes you along a winding road through forested countryside along the SS366.

---

④ Agerola

Agerola is located amid a wide green valley approximately 600m above sea level. It is surrounded by natural forests and offers amazing views of the surrounding mountains and Mediterranean Sea. Be sure to make a stop here for the legendary *fior di latte* (cow's-milk mozzarella) and *caciocavallo* (gourd-shaped traditional curd

Acerno

Montecorvino

Eboli

Battipaglia

[SP175]

Sele

Paestum ⑩ [FINISH]

Capaccio Scalo

④

Parco Nazionale del Cilento e Vallo di Diano

⑤ LINK YOUR TRIP

1 Amalfi Coast

Sorrento kicks off this weeklong adventure of hairpin turns and vertical landscapes amid the world's most glamorous stretch of coastline (p17).

2 Shadow of Vesuvius

From Sorrento, where this trip begins, head around the Bay of Naples to conquer Naples (Napoli), wander the ruins of Pompeii and Herculaneum, and brave the slopes of Vesuvius (p27).

cheese) produced on the fertile slopes around town.

The Drive ›› From Agerola to Bomerano, hop back on the SS366 for a quick 3km jaunt, enjoying a forest of beech trees and a backdrop of mountains thickly quilted with pines. You are now in the depths of the verdant Parco Regionale dei Monte Lattari.

⑤ Bomerano

Just a stone's throw from Agerola, you can easily follow your nose to tiny Bomerano for delicious buffalo-milk yogurt, an ultra-rich, mildly tangy and creamy treat. Stop by **Fusco** (Via Principe di Piemonte 3) for a tub of homemade yogurt. While there, you can also feast your eyes on the ornate ceiling frieze in the 16th-century **Chiesa San Matteo Apostolo**.

The Drive ›› From Bomerano to Conca dei Marini, continue on the same road, SS366, for 9km as it winds dramatically down to the sea, with strategically placed lookouts along the way. From the SS366, you will do more switchbacking down to the town of Conca dei Marini itself.

TRIP HIGHLIGHT

⑥ Conca dei Marini

This charmingly picturesque fishing village has been beloved by everyone from Princess Margaret to Gianni Agnelli, Jacqueline Onassis and Carlo Ponti. Work up an appetite with an excursion to the **Grotta dello Smeraldo** (Green Cavern), a seaside cavern where the waters glow an eerie emerald green. Then head back to the town for a *sfogliatella,* a scrumptious shell-shaped, ricotta-stuffed pastry that was probably invented here in the 18th century in the monastery of Santa Rosa. The local pastry is even honoured with its own holiday: the first Sunday in August.

The Drive ›› Head northeast on the SS163 to the town of Amalfi.

TRIP HIGHLIGHT

⑦ Amalfi (p92)

Gourmets shouldn't miss *scialatielli* in gorgeous little Amalfi. Shaped like short, slightly widened strips of *tagliatelle, scialatielli* is a local speciality, most commonly accompanied by zucchini and mussels or clams, or a simple sauce of fresh cherry tomatoes and garlic.

The Drive ›› It's about 15km on the SS163 from Amalfi to Cetara. Silver birches and buildings draped in bougainvillea add to the beauty of the drive.

⑧ Cetara (p103)

Tuna and anchovies are the local specialities in Cetara, a tumble-down fishing village just beyond Erchie. The sauce from anchovies

JULIUS/VLOOTHUIS/GETTY IMAGES ©

Boats in the village harbour, Cetara

DETOUR: CAPRI

Start: ❶ Sorrento

A mass of limestone rock that rises sheer through impossibly blue water, Capri is the perfect microcosm of Mediterranean appeal – a smooth cocktail of chichi piazzas and cool cafes, Roman ruins and rugged seascapes. Need any more reason to go?

OK, here's one more: the *torta caprese*. Back in the 1920s, when an absent-minded baker forgot to add flour to the mix of a cake order, a great dessert was born. Now a traditional Italian chocolate and almond or walnut cake, it is named for the island of Capri from which it originated. The cake has a thin hard shell covering a moist interior. It is usually covered with a light dusting of fine powdered sugar, and sometimes made with a small amount of Strega or other liqueur. It's even gluten-free.

Gescab-Linee Marittime Partenopee (✆081 704 19 11; www.consorziolmp.it) runs hydrofoils from Sorrento to Capri from April to November (€15, 20 minutes, 15 daily).

---

appears in various guises at Al Convento (✆089 26 10 39; www.alconvento. net; Piazza San Francesco 16; meals €25; ⊙12.30-3pm & 7-11pm summer, closed Wed winter), a first-rate seafood restaurant near the harbour. For your money, you'll probably not eat better anywhere else on the coast; the *puttanesca con alici fresche* (pasta with fresh anchovy sauce, chilli and garlic) sings with flavour.

The Drive » Head northeast on SS163 for Salerno. En route, colourful wildflowers spill over white stone walls as you travel the sometimes hair-raising 11km along the coast.

---

❾ Salerno (p104)

Salerno may seem like a bland big city after the Amalfi Coast's glut of pretty towns, but the place has a charming, if gritty, individuality, especially around its vibrant *centro storico* (historic centre). Don't miss the **cathedral** (Piazza Alfano; ⊙9am-6pm Mon-Sat, 4-6pm Sun), built in the 11th century and graced by a magnificent main entrance, the 12th-century **Porta dei Leoni**. And for *torta ricotta e pere* (ricotta and pear tart), Sorrento is the *ne plus ultra*. This dessert is an Amalfi speciality, deriving its unique tang from the local sheep's-milk ricotta.

The Drive » Head south on the SP175 and hug the coast all the way. Lush palm and lemon trees and the sparkling sea are your escorts for this 38km drive to Paestum.

TRIP HIGHLIGHT

❿ Paestum (p107)

Work up an appetite amid Paestum's fascinating **ancient ruins** (✆0828 81 10 23; incl museum adult/reduced €10/5; ⊙8.45am-7.45pm, last entry 7pm Jun & Jul, as early as 3.35pm Nov), including some of the best-preserved Greek temples in the world. Then head to **Tenuta Vannulo** (✆0828 72 47 65; www.vannulo.it; Via G Galilei Capaccio Scalo; 1hr tour €4, incl lunch €20), a 10-minute drive from Paestum, for a superbly soft and creamy mozzarella made from the organic milk of water buffalo. For a tour and lunch, reservations are essential. You can also stop just to buy the cheese, but be warned: it usually sells out by early afternoon.

Right Temple of Hera, Paestum Archaeological site

Cilento Coastal Trail

4

Following the wild and rugged coastline of the Cilento peninsula, this trip takes in pristine coastline, fascinating hilltop towns, ancient Greek ruins and atmospheric fishing villages.

TRIP HIGHLIGHTS

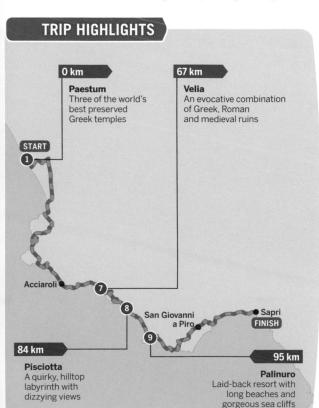

0 km

Paestum
Three of the world's best preserved Greek temples

67 km

Velia
An evocative combination of Greek, Roman and medieval ruins

START
1

Acciaroli
7
8

San Giovanni a Piro
9

Sapri
FINISH

84 km

Pisciotta
A quirky, hilltop labyrinth with dizzying views

95 km

Palinuro
Laid-back resort with long beaches and gorgeous sea cliffs

4–5 DAYS
148KM / 92 MILES

GREAT FOR...

BEST TIME TO GO
Spring and autumn for hikers; high summer for beach types.

ESSENTIAL PHOTO
Capture rugged coast and royal blue sea from hilltop Pisciotta.

BEST FOR OUTDOORS
The Palinuro peninsula, where fragrant pines meet sheer cliffs and open sea.

Left Santa Maria di Castellabate beach (p47)

45

4 Cilento Coastal Trail

Barely accessible by road until the 20th century, the jagged cliffs of the Cilento peninsula immerse you in one of Italy's least-explored stretches of coastline. After flourishing under the Greeks and Romans, the Cilento was abandoned for centuries to the vagaries of Mediterranean pirates. Today its fishing villages and pretty hill towns remain largely free of mass development, despite long strands, pristine blue waters and exquisite local seafood.

TRIP HIGHLIGHT

❶ Paestum (p107)

The three stately, honey-coloured temples at Paestum are among the best preserved in Magna Graecia – the Greek colonies that once held sway over much of southern Italy. The Greeks capitulated to the Romans in 273 BC, and Poseidonia, as it was known, remained a thriving trading port until the fall of the Roman Empire.

Tickets to the **ruins** (☎0828 81 10 23; incl museum adult/reduced €10/5; ⏱8.45am-7.45pm, last entry 7pm Jun & Jul, as early as 3.35pm Nov) are sold at the main entrance near the tourist office, or, in winter, from the museum, which features frescoes, statuary and lots of historical and archaeological insight.

The first temple you encounter after the main entrance is the 6th-century-BC **Tempio di Cerere** (Temple of Ceres). The smallest of the three temples, it served for a time as a Christian church. The sprawling site also includes remnants of the Roman city, including an amphitheatre, housing complexes and the **foro** (main square and administrative centre). Beyond lies the **Tempio di Nettuno** (Temple of Neptune), the largest and best preserved of the three temples.

LINK YOUR TRIP

3 **Southern Larder**

Join this culinary adventure through Campania where this trips begins – amid the ancient ruins of Paestum (p37).

DETOUR: PARCO NAZIONALE DEL CILENTO E VALLO DI DIANO

Start: **1** **Paestum**

Italy's second-largest national park, **Parco Nazionale del Cilento e Vallo di Diano** (www.parks. it/parco.nazionale.cilento) occupies the lion's share of the Cilento peninsula. The most interesting and accessible parts of the park lie within an hour's drive northeast of Paestum in the northwest corner of the park. The park's interior offers great opportunities for spelunking, especially the otherworldly caverns at **Grotta di Castelcivita**, near the town of Castelcivita. The town of **Sicignano degli Alburni**, capped by a medieval castle, provides a good base to hike up 1742m-high **Monte Alburno**. Finally, the medieval centre of nearby **Postiglione**, crowned by an 11th-century Norman castle, makes for a lovely stroll.

Next door, the equally beautiful **basilica** (in reality, a temple to the goddess Hera) is Paestum's oldest surviving monument, dating from the middle of the 6th century BC.

The Drive » Heading 10km south down the SP430 from Paestum, you quickly start winding into the foothills of the Cilento. Agropoli's historic centre will loom up on the right. Follow signs to the 'Centro Storico'.

---

2 Agropoli (p108)

Guarding the northern flank of the Cilento peninsula, the ancient town of Agropoli proffers stunning views across the Gulf of Salerno to the Amalfi Coast. The outskirts are made up of a rather faceless grid of shop-lined streets, but the historic kernel, occupying a rocky promontory, is a charming tangle of cobbled streets with ancient churches, the remains of a castle and superlative views up and down the coast.

The Drive » South of Agropoli, the 13km stretch of the SS267 turns inland, giving a taste of Cilento's rugged interior, but you'll quickly head west and to the sea.

---

3 Santa Maria di Castellabate (p110)

Because of the danger of sudden pirate attacks, all the coastal towns of Cilento once consisted of a low-lying coastal fishing community and a nearby highly defended hilltop town where peasants and fishermen could find quick refuge.

These days, the fishing district of Castellabate – known as Santa Maria di Castellabate – has outgrown its hilltop protector, thanks to the town's 4km stretch of golden-sand beach. Despite the development, the town's historic centre preserves a palpable southern Italian feel, with dusky-pink and ochre houses blinkered by traditional green shutters. The little harbour is especially charming, with its 19th-century *palazzi* and the remnants of a much older castle. Note that these charms can diminish quickly when summer crowds overwhelm the scant parking.

The Drive » Just past the town of Santa Maria di Castellabate along SS267 is the turn-off to Castellabate. The road then winds through orchards and olive groves for 8km.

4 Castellabate (p110)

With sweeping sea views, medieval Castellabate clings to the top of a steep hill 280m above sea level. One of the most endearing and historic towns on the Cilento coast, its strategic location helped defend residents from pirate

incursions throughout the Middle Ages. Its labyrinth of narrow pedestrian streets is punctuated by ancient archways, small piazzas and the occasional *palazzo*.

The Drive » Head back down to the SS267 and follow for 21km, which turns inland once again, but you will see the sea soon enough as you twist down to Acciaroli.

5 Acciaroli (p110)

Despite a growing number of concrete resorts on its outskirts, the tastefully restored historic centre of this fishing village makes it worth a stop, especially for Hemingway lovers. The author spent time here in the 1940s, and some say he based his *The Old Man and the Sea* on a local fisherman.

The Drive » After Acciaroli, the coastal highway climbs quickly for 8km to Pioppi, proffering stunning views down the Cilento coast to Capo Palinuro.

6 Pioppi (p110)

Tiny, seaside Pioppi has the right to feel smug. Based on observations of this town's vigorous older residents in the late 1950s, American medical researcher Dr Ancel Keys launched his famous study concerning the health benefits of

the Mediterranean diet. Join a new generation of geezers dozing on the shady benches of lovely Piazza de Millenario. Suitably rested, take a picnic to the pristine, pale pebble beach a few steps away.

The Drive » By Cilento standards, it's practically a straight shot for 7km along the coastal highway to the town of Ascea, where coastal mountains make way for the small but rich plains that once fed ancient Velia.

7 Velia

Founded by the Greeks in the mid-6th century BC, and subsequently a popular resort for wealthy Romans, Velia (formerly Elea) was once home to philosophers Parmenides and Zeno. Today you can wander around the town's evocative **ruins** (☏0974 97 23 96; Ascea; adult/reduced €2/1; ☺9am-1hr before sunset Mon-Sat), including intact portions of the original city walls, plus remnants of thermal baths, an Ionic temple, a Roman theatre and even a medieval castle.

The Drive » You are now headed into the most hair-raising stretch of the Cilento's coastal highway, but spectacular views are your reward. Olive trees start multiplying as you near Pisciotta. The total distance is about 24km.

Right Port of Acciaroli

ROBANGEL69/GETTY IMAGES ©

8 Pisciotta (p110)

The liveliest town in the Cilento and also its most dramatic, hilltop Pisciotta consists of a steeply pitched maze of medieval streets. Life centres on the lively main square where the town's largely elderly residents rule the roost. The hills surrounding the town are terraced into rich olive groves and produce particularly prized oil, while local fishermen specialise in anchovies. When their catch is marinated in the local oil, the result is mouthwateringly good.

The Drive >> The 15km trip begins with a steep descent from Pisciotta, and a straight road to Palinuro. Before reaching town, you'll see its beautiful, miles-long beach.

9 Palinuro (p112)

The Cilento's main resort, Palinuro remains remarkably low-key (and low rise), with a tangible fishing-village feel, though its beaches become crowded in August. Extending past its postcard-pretty harbour, the remarkable 2km-long promontory known as **Capo Palinuro** proffers wonderful walking trails and views up and down the coast.

Better yet, you can visit its sea cliffs and hidden caves, including Palinuro's own version of Capri's famous Grotta Azzurra, with a similarly spectacular display of water, colour and light. To arrange the 90-minute excursion, contact **Da Alessandro** (✆347 654 09 31; www.costieradelcilento.it; trips from €15).

The Drive >> Begin the 27km drive with a beautiful jaunt along the water before heading inland at Marina di Camerota. Get ready for plenty of sharp turns as you wind up stunning SS562.

10 San Giovanni a Piro

With its tight-knit historic centre and jaw-dropping views across

The Cilento coastline

the Gulf of Policastro to the mountains of La Basilicata and Calabria, this little agricultural town makes a worthy stop as you wind your way around the wild, southern tip of the Cilento peninsula.

The Drive » The final 30km of this trip begins with a winding descent from San Giovanni a Piro to the pretty port town of Scario; the road flattens out as you make your way around the picturesque Golfo di Policastro.

- - - - - - - - - - - -

⑪ Sapri

Set on an almost perfectly round natural harbour, Sapri is the ideal place to wave goodbye to the Cilento. The peninsula's dramatic interior mountains rear up across the beautiful Golfo di Policastro. Admire the views from the town's seafront promenade or from one of its nearby beaches.

Destinations

Naples & Pompeii (p54)

Naples explodes with art and antiquities, from colossal Roman statues at Museo Archeologico Nazionale to Caravaggio at Palazzo Reale di Capodimonte.

Sorrento & Around (p72)

A strangely appealing place, Sorrento oozes laid-back southern-Italian charm.

The Amalfi Coast (p85)

The Amalfi Coast (Costiera Amalfitana) is one of Europe's most breathtaking.

Salerno & the Cilento (p104)

Salerno is an intriguing labyrinth of colourful earthy streets, which makes for a refreshing change from the more touristy towns to the west.

Positano (p85)

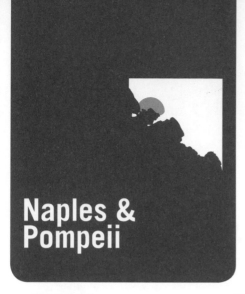

Blessed with rich volcanic soils, a bountiful sea and centuries of culinary know-how, the Naples region is one of Italy's epicurean heavyweights, serving up the country's best pizza, pasta and coffee, and many of its most celebrated seafood dishes, street snacks and sweet treats.

Naples & Pompeii

NAPLES

POP 989,110

Italy's third-largest city is one of its oldest, most artistic and most delicious. Naples' *centro storico* (historic centre) is a Unesco World Heritage Site, its archaeological treasures are among the world's most impressive, and its swag of vainglorious palaces, castles and churches make Rome look positively provincial.

Certainly, Naples' urban sprawl can feel anarchic, tattered and unloved. But look beyond the grime and graffiti and you'll uncover a city of breathtaking frescoes, sculptures and panoramas, of unexpected elegance, of spontaneous conversations and profound humanity.

⊙ Sights

⊙ Centro Storico

★**Complesso Monumentale di Santa Chiara**　　BASILICA, MONASTERY
(☑081 551 66 73; www.monasterodisantachiara. eu; Via Santa Chiara 49c; basilica free, Complesso Monumentale adult/reduced €6/4.50; ⊙basilica 7.30am-1pm & 4.30-8pm, Complesso Monumentale 9.30am-5.30pm Mon-Sat, 10am-2.30pm Sun; Ⓜ Dante) Vast, Gothic and cleverly deceptive, the mighty **Basilica di Santa Chiara** stands at the heart of this tranquil monastery complex. The church was severely damaged in WWII: what you see today is a 20th-century recreation of Gagliardo Primario's 14th-century original. Adjoining it are the basilica's cloisters, adorned with brightly coloured 17th-century majolica tiles and frescoes.

★**Cappella Sansevero**　　CHAPEL
(☑081 551 84 70; www.museosansevero.it; Via Francesco de Sanctis 19; adult/reduced €7/5; ⊙9.30am-6.30pm Mon & Wed-Sat, to 2pm Sun; Ⓜ Dante) It's in this Masonic-inspired baroque chapel that you'll find Giuseppe Sanmartino's incredible sculpture, *Cristo velato* (Veiled Christ), its marble veil so realistic that it's tempting to try to lift it and view Christ underneath. It's one of several artistic wonders that include Francesco Queirolo's sculpture *Disinganno* (Disillusion), Antonio Corradini's *Pudicizia* (Modesty) and riotously colourful frescoes by Francesco Maria Russo, the latter untouched since their creation in 1749.

Complesso Monumentale di San Lorenzo Maggiore　　ARCHAEOLOGICAL SITE
(☑081 211 08 60; www.sanlorenzomaggiorenapoli. it; Via dei Tribunali 316; church admission free, excavations & museum adult/reduced €9/7; ⊙9.30am-5.30pm; 🚌C55 to Via Duomo) Architecture and

PLAN YOUR ROUTE
••••••••••••••••••••••••••••••••
2 **Shadow of Vesuvius** (p27)
Starting in Naples, this trip takes in some of the world's most spectacular ruins in Herculaneum and Pompeii.

NAPLES IN...

Two Days

Start with a burst of colour in the cloister of the **Basilica di Santa Chiara**, get breathless over the astounding *Cristo velato* (Veiled Christ) in the **Cappella Sansevero**, then head underground on a **Napoli Sotterranea** tour (p58). After lunch, take in Lanfranco's dome fresco in the Duomo, meditate on a Caravaggio masterpiece at **Pio Monte della Misericordia**, then simply kick back in bohemian Piazza Bellini. Next morning, explore ancient treasures at the **Museo Archeologico Nazionale**, then head up to the **Certosa e Museo di San Martino** (p56), for extraordinary baroque interiors, Neapolitan art and a sweeping panorama. Cap the night on the fashionable, bar-packed streets of Chiaia.

Four Days

Spend the morning of day three cheek-to-crater with **Mt Vesuvius** (p66), then ponder its bone-chilling fury at **Herculaneum** (p65) or **Pompeii** (p66). On day four, head up to the **Palazzo Reale di Capodimonte** (p57) to eye up the bounty of artistic masterpieces inside, then head underground on a guided tour of the otherworldly Catacomba di San Gennaro. Top it all off with a romantic evening shouting 'bravo' at the luscious **Teatro San Carlo** (p64).

history buffs shouldn't miss this richly layered religious complex, its commanding basilica deemed one of Naples' finest medieval buildings. Aside from Ferdinando Sanfelice's petite facade, the Cappella al Rosario and the Cappellone di Sant'Antonio, its baroque makeover was stripped away last century to reveal its austere, Gothic elegance. Beneath the basilica, a sprawl of extraordinary ruins will transport you back two millennia.

Pio Monte

della Misericordia CHURCH, MUSEUM

(☑ 081 44 69 44; www.piomontedellamisericordia.it; Via dei Tribunali 253; adult/reduced €7/5; ☺ 9am-2pm Thu-Tue; ☐ C55 to Via Duomo) The 1st floor of this octagonal, 17th-century church delivers a small, satisfying collection of Renaissance and baroque art, including works by Francesco de Mura, Giuseppe de Ribera, Andrea Vaccaro and Paul van Somer. It's also home to contemporary artworks by Italian and foreign artists, each inspired by Caravaggio's masterpiece *Le Sette Opere di Misericordia* (The Seven Acts of Mercy), considered by many to be the most important painting in Naples. You'll find it above the main altar in the ground-floor chapel.

★ Duomo CATHEDRAL

(☑ 081 44 90 65; Via Duomo 149; baptistry €1.50; ☺ cathedral 8.30am-1.30pm & 2.30-8pm Mon-Sat, 8.30am-1.30pm & 4.30-7.30pm Sun, baptistry 8.30am-1pm Mon-Sat, 8.30am-12.30pm & 5-6.30pm

Sun; ☐ C55 to Via Duomo) Whether you go for Giovanni Lanfranco's fresco in the **Cappella di San Gennaro** (Chapel of St Janarius), the 4th-century mosaics in the baptistry, or the thrice-annual miracle of San Gennaro, do not miss Naples' cathedral. Kick-started by Charles I of Anjou in 1272 and consecrated in 1315, it was largely destroyed in a 1456 earthquake, and has had copious nips and tucks over the subsequent centuries.

MADRE GALLERY

(Museo d'Arte Contemporanea Donnaregina; ☑ 081 1931 3016; www.madrenapoli.it; Via Settembrini 79; adult/reduced €7/3.50, Mon free; ☺ 10am-7.30pm Mon & Wed-Sat, to 8pm Sun; Ⓜ Piazza Cavour) When *Madonna and Child* overload hits, reboot at Naples' museum of modern and contemporary art. Start on level 3 – the setting for temporary exhibitions – before hitting the permanent collection of painting, sculpture and installations from prolific 20th- and 21st-century artists on level 2. Among these are Olafur Eliasson, Shirin Neshat and Julian Beck, as well as Italian heavyweights Mario Merz and Michelangelo Pistoletto. Specially commissioned installations from the likes of Francesco Clemente, Anish Kapoor and Rebecca Horn cap things off on level 1.

★ Museo Archeologico Nazionale MUSEUM

(☑ 081 442 21 49; http://cir.campania.beniculturali.it/ museoarcheologiconazionale; Piazza Museo Nazionale 19; adult/reduced €8/4; ☺ 9am-7.30pm Wed-Mon;

Ⓜ Museo, Piazza Cavour) Naples' National Archaeological Museum serves up one of the world's finest collections of Graeco-Roman artefacts. Originally a cavalry barracks and later a seat of the city's university, the museum was established by the Bourbon king Charles VII in the late 18th century to house the antiquities he inherited from his mother, Elisabetta Farnese, as well as treasures looted from Pompeii and Herculaneum. Star exhibits include the celebrated *Toro Farnese* (Farnese Bull) sculpture and a series of awe-inspiring mosaics from Pompeii's Casa del Fauno.

Before tackling the collection, consider investing in the *National Archaeological Museum of Naples* (€12), published by Electa; if you want to concentrate on the highlights, audioguides (€5) are available in English. It's also worth calling ahead to ensure that the galleries you want to see are open, as staff shortages often mean that sections of the museum close for part of the day.

◉ Vomero

★ Certosa e Museo di San Martino
MONASTERY, MUSEUM

(🖉 081 229 45 68; www.polomusealenapoli.beni culturali.it; Largo San Martino 5; adult/reduced €6/3; ◷ 8.30am-7.30pm Thu-Tue; Ⓜ Vanvitelli, Ⓕ Montesanto to Morghen) The high point (quite literally) of the Neapolitan baroque, this charterhouse-turned-museum was founded as a Carthusian monastery in the 14th century. Centred on one of the most beautiful cloisters in Italy, it has been decorated, adorned and altered over the centuries by some of Italy's finest talent, most importantly Giovanni Antonio Dosio in the 16th century and baroque master Cosimo Fanzago a century later. Nowadays it's a superb repository of Neapolitan artistry.

The monastery's church and the rooms that flank it contain a feast of frescoes and paintings by some of Naples' greatest 17th-century artists, among them Francesco Solimena, Massimo Stanzione, Giuseppe de Ribera and Battista Caracciolo. In the nave, Cosimo Fanzago's inlaid marble work is simply extraordinary.

You will need to book in advance to access the Certosa's imposing **Sotterranei Gotici** (Gothic basement), open to the public on Saturday and Sunday at 11.30am (with guided tour in Italian) and 4.30pm (without guided tour). The austere vaulted space is home to about 150 marble sculptures and epigraphs, including a statue of St Francis of Assisi by 18th-century master sculptor Giuseppe Sanmartino. To book a visit, email accoglienza. sanmartino@beniculturali.it at least two weeks in advance.

◉ Santa Lucia & Chiaia

Palazzo Reale
PALACE, MUSEUM

(Royal Palace; 🖉 081 40 05 47; www.sbapsae. na.it/cms; Piazza del Plebiscito 1; adult/reduced €4/3; ◷ 9am-8pm Thu-Tue; 🚇 R2 to Via San Carlo, Ⓜ Municipio) Envisaged as a 16th-century monument to Spanish glory (Naples was under Spanish rule at the time), the magnificent Palazzo Reale is home to the **Museo del Palazzo Reale**, a rich and eclectic collection of baroque and neoclassical furnishings, porcelain, tapestries, sculpture and paintings, spread across the palace's royal apartments.

Among the many highlights is the Teatrino di Corte, a lavish private theatre created by Ferdinando Fuga in 1768 to celebrate the marriage of Ferdinand IV and Marie Caroline of Austria. Incredibly, Angelo Viva's statues of Apollo and the Muses set along the walls are made of papier mâché.

ⓘ BEFORE YOU EXPLORE

If you're planning to blitz the sights, the **Campania Artecard** (🖉 800 60 06 01; www. campaniartecard.it) is an excellent investment. A cumulative ticket that covers museum admission and transport, it comes in various forms. The Naples three-day ticket (adult/ reduced €21/12) gives free admission to three participating sites, a 50% discount on others and free use of public transport in the city. Other handy options include a 7-day 'Tutta la Regione' ticket (€34), which offers free admission to five sites and discounted admission to others in areas as far afield as Caserta, Ravello (Amalfi Coast) and Paestum. The latter does not cover transport. Cards can be purchased online, at the dedicated Artecard booth inside the tourist office at Stazione Centrale, or at participating sites and museums.

The Cappella Reale (Royal Chapel) houses an 18th-century *presepe napoletano* (Neapolitan nativity crib). Fastidiously detailed, its cast of *pastori* (crib figurines) were crafted by a series of celebrated Neapolitan artists, including Giuseppe Sanmartino, creator of the *Cristo velato* (Veiled Christ) sculpture in the Cappella Sansevero.

The palace is also home to the **Biblioteca Nazionale** (National Library; ☑081 781 91 11; www.bnnonline.it; ⊙8.30am-7pm Mon-Fri, to 2pm Sat, papyrus exhibition closes 2pm Mon-Sat; ☐R2 to Via San Carlo, Ⓜ Municipio) **FREE**, its own priceless treasures including at least 2000 papyri discovered at Herculaneum and fragments of a 5th-century Coptic Bible. Bring photo ID to enter the Biblioteca Nazionale.

Castel Nuovo   CASTLE, MUSEUM
(☑081 795 77 22; Piazza Municipio; admission €6; ⊙9am-7pm Mon-Sat, last entry 6pm; Ⓜ Municipio) Locals know this 13th-century castle as the Maschio Angioino (Angevin Keep) and its Cappella Palatina is home to fragments of frescoes by Renaissance maverick Giotto; they're on the splays of the Gothic windows. You'll find Roman ruins under the glass-floored Sala dell'Armeria (Armoury Hall), and a collection of mostly 17th- to early-20th-century Neapolitan paintings on the upper floors. The top floor houses the more interesting works, including landscape paintings by Luigi Crisconio and a watercolour drawing by architect Carlo Vanvitelli.

◎ Capodimonte & La Sanità

★**Palazzo Reale di Capodimonte**   MUSEUM
(☑081 749 91 11; www.polomusealenapoli.beni culturali.it; Via Miano 2; adult/reduced €7.50/3.75; ⊙8.30am-7.30pm Thu-Tue; ☐R4, 178 to Via Capodimonte) Originally designed as a hunting lodge for Charles VII of Bourbon, this monumental palace was begun in 1738 and took more than a century to complete. It's now home to the **Museo Nazionale di Capodimonte**, southern Italy's largest and richest art gallery. Its vast collection – much of which Charles inherited from his mother, Elisabetta Farnese – was moved here in 1759 and ranges from exquisite 12th-century altar-pieces to works by Botticelli, Caravaggio, Titian and Andy Warhol.

The gallery is spread over three floors and 160 rooms; for most people, a full morning or afternoon is enough for an abridged best-of tour. The 1st floor includes works by

greats such as Michelangelo, Raphael and Titian, with highlights including Masaccio's *Crocifissione* (Crucifixion; Room 3), Botticelli's *Madonna col Bambino e due angeli* (Madonna with Child and Angels; Room 6), Bellini's *Trasfigurazione* (Transfiguration; Room 8) and Parmigianino's *Antea* (Room 12). The floor is also home to the royal apartments, a study in regal excess. The **Salottino di Porcellana** (Room 52) is an outrageous example of 18th-century chinoiserie, its walls and ceiling dense with whimsically themed porcelain 'stucco'. Originally created between 1757 and 1759 for the Palazzo Reale in Portici, it was transferred to Capodimonte in 1867.

Upstairs, the 2nd-floor galleries display work by Neapolitan artists from the 13th to the 19th centuries, including de Ribera, Giordano, Solimena and Stanzione. The piece that many come to see, however, is Caravaggio's *Flagellazione* (Flagellation; 1607–10), which hangs in reverential solitude in Room 78.

If you have any energy left, the small gallery of modern art on the 3rd floor is worth a quick look, if for nothing else than Andy Warhol's poptastic *Mt Vesuvius*.

Once you've finished in the museum, the **Parco di Capodimonte** – the palace's 130-hectare estate – provides a much-needed breath of fresh air.

Cimitero delle Fontanelle   CEMETERY
(☑081 1970 3197; cimiterofontanelle.com; Via Fontanelle 80; ⊙9am-4pm; ☐C51 to Via Fontanelle) **FREE** Holding about eight million human bones, the ghoulish Fontanelle Cemetery was first used during the 1656 plague, before becoming Naples' main burial site during the 1837 cholera epidemic. At the end of the 19th century it became a hot spot for the *anime pezzentelle* (poor souls) cult, in which locals adopted skulls and prayed for their souls. Lack of information at the site makes joining a tour much more rewarding; reputable outfits include Cooperativa Sociale Onlus 'La Paranza'.

⚐ Tours

Tunnel Borbonico   HISTORIC SITE
(☑081 764 58 08, 366 2484151; www.tunnelbor bonico.info; Vico del Grottone 4; 75min standard tour adult/reduced €10/5; ⊙standard tour 10am, noon, 3.30pm & 5.30pm Fri-Sun; ☐R2 to Via San Carlo) Traverse five centuries along Naples' engrossing Bourbon Tunnel. Conceived by Ferdinand II in 1853 to link the Palazzo Reale to the barracks and the sea, the

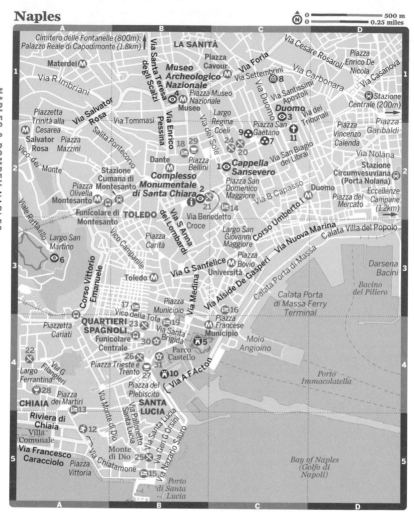

never-completed escape route is part of the 17th-century Carmignano Aqueduct system, itself incorporating 16th-century cisterns. An air-raid shelter and military hospital during WWII, this underground labyrinth rekindles the past with evocative wartime artefacts. The standard tour doesn't require booking, though the Adventure Tour (80 minutes; adult/reduced €15/10) and adults-only Speleo Tour (2½ hours; €30) do. Tours also depart from Tunnel Borbonico's second entrance, reached through the Parcheggio Morelli (Via Domenico Morelli 40) parking complex in Chiaia.

Napoli Sotterranea ARCHAEOLOGICAL SITE
(Underground Naples; ☏ 081 29 69 44; www. napolisotterranea.org; Piazza San Gaetano 68; adult/reduced €10/8; ☺ English tours 10am, noon, 2pm, 4pm & 6pm; 🚌 C55 to Via Duomo) This evocative guided tour leads you 40m below street level to explore Naples' ancient labyrinth of aqueducts, passages and cisterns.

★★ Festivals & Events

Festa di San Gennaro RELIGIOUS
The faithful flock to the Duomo to witness the miraculous liquefaction of San Gennaro's blood on the Saturday before the first Sunday

Naples

in May. Repeat performances take place on 19 September and 16 December.

Maggio dei Monumenti   CULTURAL
(☺May) A month-long cultural feast, with concerts, performances, exhibitions, guided tours and other events across Naples.

🛏 Sleeping

B&B Cappella Vecchia   B&B €
(☑081 240 51 17; www.cappellavecchia11.it; Vico Santa Maria a Cappella Vecchia 11; s €50-80, d €75-110, tr €90-140; ✴@🛜; 🚇C24 to Piazza dei Martiri) Run by a super-helpful young couple, this B&B is a first-rate choice in the smart, fashionable Chiaia district. Rooms are simple and upbeat, with funky bathrooms, vibrant colours, and Neapolitan themes. There's a spacious communal area for breakfast, and free internet available 24/7. Check the website for special offers.

Hostel of the Sun   HOSTEL €
(☑081 420 63 93; www.hostelnapoli.com; Via G Melisurgo 15; dm €18-22, s €30-35, d €60-80; ✴@🛜; 🚇Municipio) HOTS is an ultra-friendly hostel near the hydrofoil and ferry terminals. Located on the 7th floor (have €0.05 for the lift), it's a bright, sociable place with multicoloured dorms, a casual in-house bar (with cheap cocktails between 8pm and 11pm) and – a few floors down – a series of hotel-standard private rooms, seven with en-suite bathrooms.

★**Hotel Piazza Bellini**   BOUTIQUE HOTEL €€
(☑081 45 17 32; www.hotelpiazzabellini.com; Via Santa Maria di Costantinopoli 101; d from €100; ✴@🛜; 🚇Dante) Only steps from buzzing Piazza Bellini, this sharp, contemporary hotel occupies a 16th-century *palazzo,* its mint white spaces spiked with original majolica tiles and the work of emerging artists. Rooms offer pared-back cool, with designer fittings, chic bathrooms and mirror frames drawn straight onto the wall. Rooms on the 5th and 6th floors have panoramic terraces.

**Decumani Hotel
de Charme**   BOUTIQUE HOTEL €€
(☑081 551 81 88; www.decumani.it; Via San Giovanni Maggiore Pignatelli 15; s €99-124, d €99-164; ✴@🛜; 🚇Università) This classic boutique hotel occupies the former *palazzo* of Cardinal Sisto Riario Sforza, the last bishop of the Bourbon kingdom. Simple, stylish rooms feature high ceilings, parquet floors, 19th-century furniture, and modern bathrooms with spacious showers. Deluxe rooms crank up *la dolce vita* with personal hot tubs. The *pièce de résistance*, however, is the property's breathtaking baroque salon.

**La Ciliegina
Lifestyle Hotel**   BOUTIQUE HOTEL €€
(☑081 1971 8800; www.cilieginahotel.it; Via PE Imbriani 30; d €150-250, junior ste €200-350; ✴@🛜; 🚇Municipio) An easy walk from the hydrofoil terminal, this chic, contemporary

slumber spot is a hit with fashion-conscious urbanites. Spacious white rooms are splashed with blue and red accents, each with top-of-the-range Hästens bed, flat-screen TV and marble-clad bathroom with water-jet Jacuzzi shower (one junior suite has a Jacuzzi tub).

Hotel Il Convento   HOTEL €€

(☑081 40 39 77; www.hotelilconvento.com; Via Speranzella 137a; s €50-93, d €65-140; ❋ 🗟; Ⓜ Municipio) This lovely hotel in the Quartieri Spagnoli is a soothing blend of antique Tuscan furniture, well-stocked bookshelves and candle-lit stairs. Rooms are cosy and elegant, combining creamy tones and dark woods with patches of 16th-century brickwork. For €80 to €180 you get a room with a private roof garden. The hotel is wheelchair accessible.

Grand Hotel Vesuvio   HOTEL €€€

(☑081 764 00 44; www.vesuvio.it; Via Partenope 45; s/d €280/310; ❋ @ 🗟; 🚌128 to Via Santa Lucia) Known for hosting legends – past guests include Rita Hayworth and Humphrey Bogart – this five-star heavyweight is a decadent mélange of dripping chandeliers, period antiques and opulent rooms. Count your lucky stars while drinking a martini at the rooftop restaurant.

✗ Eating

Pizza and pasta are the staples of Neapolitan cuisine. Pizza was created here and nowhere will you eat it better. Seafood is another local speciality and you'll find mussels and clams served in many dishes. Neapolitan street food is equally delicious. *Misto di frittura* – zucchini flowers, deep-fried potato and aubergine – makes for a great snack, especially if eaten from paper outside a tiny streetside stall. It's always sensible to book a table if dining at a restaurant on a Friday or Saturday night. Also note that many eateries close for two to four weeks in August, so check before heading out.

★ Pizzeria Gino Sorbillo   PIZZA €

(☑081 44 66 43; www.accademiadellapizza.it; Via dei Tribunali 32; pizzas from €3.30; ☉noon-3.30pm & 7pm-1am Mon-Sat; Ⓜ Dante) Day in, day out, this cult-status pizzeria is besieged by hungry hordes. While debate may rage over whether Gino Sorbillo's pizzas are the best in town, there's no doubt that his giant, wood-fired discs – made using organic flour

and tomatoes – will have you licking finger tips and whiskers. Head in super early or prepare to queue.

La Campagnola   NEAPOLITAN €

(☑081 45 90 34; Via dei Tribunali 47; meals €18; ☉12.30-4pm & 7-11.30pm; 🗟; Ⓜ Dante) Boisterous and affable, this spruced-up Neapolitan stalwart dishes unfussed, soul-coaxing classics. Daily specials include a killer *genovese* (pasta with a slow-cooked lamb, tomato and onion *ragù*) on Thursday, while week-round classics include hearty *salsiccia con friarielli* (pork sausage with Neapolitan bitter greens). If there's still room to move, conclude with the rum-soaked *babà*.

Pintauro   PASTRIES €

(☑348 7781645; Via Toledo 275; sfogliatelle €2; ☉9am-8pm Mon-Sat, 9.30am-2pm Sun, closed mid-Jul–early Sep; 🚌R2 to Via San Carlo, Ⓜ Municipio) Of Neapolitan *dolci* (sweets), the cream of the crop is the *sfogliatella,* a shell of flaky pastry stuffed with creamy, scented ricotta. This local institution has been selling *sfogliatelle* since the early 1800s, when its founder supposedly brought them to Naples from their culinary birthplace on the Amalfi Coast.

La Taverna di Santa Chiara   NEAPOLITAN €€

(☑339 8150346; Via Santa Chiara 6; meals €25; ☉12.30-3pm & 7-11pm Wed-Mon; 🗟; Ⓜ Dante) Gragnano pasta, Agerola pork, Benevento *latte nobile:* this intimate, two-level eatery is healthily obsessed with small, local producers and Slow Food ingredients. The result is a beautiful, seasonal journey across Campania. For an inspiring overview, order the *antipasto misto* (mixed antipasto), then tuck into lesser-known classics like *zuppa di soffritto* (spicy meat stew) with a glass of smooth house *vino.*

★ Eccellenze Campane   NEAPOLITAN €€

(☑081 20 36 57; www.eccellenzecampane.it; Via Benedetto Brin 49; pizza from €6, meals €30; ☉7am-11pm Sun-Fri, to midnight Sat; 🚌116, 192, 460, 472, 475) This is Naples' answer to Turin-based food emporium Eataly, an impressive, contemporary showcase for top-notch Campanian comestibles. The sprawling space is divided into various dining and shopping sections, offering everything from beautifully charred pizzas and light *fritture* (fried snacks) to finer-dining seafood, coveted Sal Da Riso pastries, craft beers and no shortage of take-home pantry treats. A must for gastronomes.

Trattoria San Ferdinando
NEAPOLITAN €€

(☎081 42 19 64; Via Nardones 117; meals €27; ⊙noon-3pm Mon-Sat, 7.30-11pm Tue-Fri; ☐R2 to Via San Carlo, ⓜMunicipio) Hung with theatre posters, cosy San Ferdinando pulls in well-spoken theatre types and intellectuals. For a Neapolitan taste trip, ask for a rundown of the day's antipasti and choose your favourites for an *antipasto misto* (mixed antipasto). Seafood standouts include a delicate *seppia ripieno* (stuffed squid), while the homemade desserts make for a satisfying dénouement.

★ L'Ebbrezza di Noè
NEAPOLITAN €€

(☎081 40 01 04; www.lebbrezzadinoe.com; Vico Vetriera 9; meals €37; ⊙8.30pm-midnight Tue-Sun; ⓜPiazza Amedeo) A wine shop by day, 'Noah's Drunkenness' transforms into an intimate culinary hot spot by night. Slip inside for *vino* and conversation at the bar, or settle into one of the bottle-lined dining rooms for seductive, market-driven dishes like house special *paccheri fritti* (fried pasta stuffed with aubergine and served with fresh basil and a rich tomato sauce).

Ristorantino dell'Avvocato
NEAPOLITAN €€

(☎081 032 00 47; www.ilristorantinodellavvocato. it; Via Santa Lucia 115-117; meals €40; ⊙noon-3pm & 7.30-11pm, lunch only Mon & Sun; 🛜; ☐128 to Via Santa Lucia) This elegant yet welcoming restaurant has quickly won the respect of Neapolitan gastronomes. Apple of their eye is affable lawyer turned head chef Raffaele Cardillo, whose passion for Campania's culinary heritage merges with a knack for subtle, refreshing twists – think gnocchi with fresh mussels, clams, crumbed pistachio, lemon, ginger and garlic.

🍷 Drinking & Nightlife

Caffè Gambrinus
CAFE

(☎081 41 75 82; www.grancaffegambrinus.com; Via Chiaia 12; ⊙7am-1am Sun-Thu, to 2am Fri, to 3am Sat; ☐R2 to Via San Carlo, ⓜMunicipio) Grand, chandeliered Gambrinus is Naples' oldest and most venerable cafe. Oscar Wilde knocked back a few here and Mussolini had some of the rooms shut to keep out left-wing intellectuals. The prices may be steep, but the *aperitivo* nibbles are decent and sipping a *spritz* or a luscious *cioccolata calda* (hot chocolate) in its belle époque rooms is something worth savouring.

Spazio Nea
CAFE

(☎081 45 13 58; www.spazionea.it; Via Constantinopoli 53; ⊙9am-2am; 🛜; ⓜDante) Aptly skirting bohemian Piazza Bellini, this white-washed gallery features its own cafe-bar speckled with books, flowers, cultured crowds and alfresco seating at the bottom of a baroque staircase. Eye up exhibitions of contemporary Italian and foreign art, then kick back with a *caffé* or a Cynar *spritz*. Check Nea's Facebook page for upcoming readings, live music gigs or DJ sets.

Authentic Neapolitan pizza

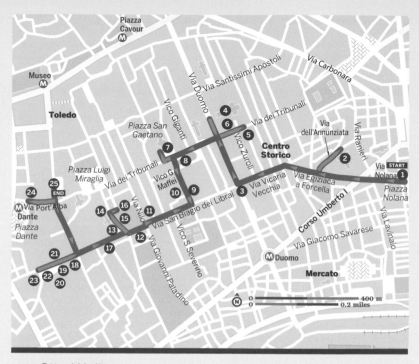

🏃 City Walk
Centro Storico: A World Heritage Wander

START PORTA NOLANA
END PIAZZA BELLINI
LENGTH 3KM; FOUR HOURS

Bustling for over 2000 years, Naples' *centro historico* (historic centre) is a rumbling mass of contradictions. Hyperactive streets sit atop silent ruins, crumbling facades mask mighty baroque interiors, and cultish shrines flank hedonistic bars. No other part of the city intrigues or intoxicates so intensely, and none offers such a density of artistic and architectural treasures.

Begin your walk at 15th-century city gate ❶ **Porta Nolana**, its exterior wall featuring a marble relief of Ferdinand I, illegitimate son of Alfonso V of Aragon (who was also king of Naples from 1458 to 1494). On the other side of the gate is a 17th-century bust of San Gaetano. These days, Porta Nolana is better known as the gateway to the Mercato di Porta Nolana.

After exploring the market, head west along Via Nolana. Cross Corso Umberto I, head right into Via Egiziaca a Forcella and then right again into Via dell'Annunziata. A little way down on your right you'll see the ❷ **Santissima Annunziata**, famous for its orphanage and *ruota*, the wooden wheel where babies were once abandoned. Head back to Via Egiziaca a Forcella and turn right into it. After crossing Via Pietro Colletta, follow the street as it veers left and merges into Via Vicaria Vecchia. Where it meets Via Duomo stands one of Naples' oldest churches, the ❸ **Basilica di San Giorgio Maggiore**. Built by St Severus in the 4th century but thoroughly restyled by Cosimo Fanzago in the mid-17th century, its original Palaeo-Christian apse is now part of the main entrance. Two blocks northwest up Via Duomo soars Naples' impressive cathedral, the ❹ **Duomo** (p55).

Double back down Via Duomo until you meet Via dei Tribunali. Known to the Romans as the *decumanus maior* (main road), this street runs parallel to the *decumanus inferior*, aka Spaccanapoli, aka Via San Biagio dei Librai. Before heading right into the heart of the *centro storico*, nip left to admire Caravaggio's masterpiece *Le Sette Opere di Misericordia* (The Seven Acts of Mercy) in the ❺ **Pio Monte della Misericordia** (p55). Soaring from the small square opposite is the ❻ **Guglia di San Gennaro**.

After you've crossed Via Duomo make for Piazza San Gaetano, about 150m down on the right. The tiny square where the Roman forum once stood is now dominated by the imposing ❼ **Basilica di San Paolo Maggiore**, whose sumptuous baroque sacristy is one of the city's hidden delights. Opposite the piazza is the ❽ **Complesso Monumentale di San Lorenzo Maggiore** (p54), its stark but beautiful Gothic basilica sitting atop evocative Roman *scavi* (excavations). Take a peek before heading down ❾ **Via San Gregorio Armeno** – in December people come from all over Italy to visit the *presepi* (nativity scene) shops that line this street. Also here is the rococo ❿ **Chiesa e Chiostro di San Gregorio Armeno**.

At the end of the road you hit Via San Biagio dei Librai. Turn right and after about 250m you'll be on ⓫ **Piazzetta Nilo**, home to the ancient Statua del Nilo and (less imposingly) the altar to footballer Maradona inside Bar Nilo. Further down on the left, the ⓬ **Chiesa di Sant'Angolo a Nilo** is home to an exquisite tomb.

From here it's only a few steps to handsome ⓭ **Piazza San Domenico Maggiore**, location of the imposing ⓮ **Chiesa di San Domenico Maggiore**. At No 9 stands the notorious ⓯ **Palazzo dei Di Sangro**, where

composer Carlo Gesualdo brutally murdered his wife and her lover. Around the corner from the *palazzo* is Via Francesco de Sanctis, where you'll find the not-to-be-missed ⓰ **Cappella Sansevero** (p54), home to the mesmerising *Cristo velato* (Veiled Christ).

As you walk west on Via San Biagio dei Librai it becomes Via Benedetto Croce. On the left, at No 45, stands ⓱ **Palazzo Carafa della Spina**, designed by Domenico Fontana in the late 16th century and revamped in the first half of the 18th century. Its baroque *portone* (entrance) is one of Naples' finest. Further west is the ⓲ **Basilica di Santa Chiara** (p54), meticulously reconstructed after heavy bomb damage in WWII. Nearby ⓳ **Piazza del Gesù Nuovo** is home to nightly revelry and, at No 14, ⓴ **Libreria Dante & Descartes**, an erudite bookshop. Dominating the piazza's northern side is the glorious ㉑ **Chiesa del Gesù Nuovo**, while at its centre is the ㉒ **Guglia dell'Immacolata**, created between 1747 and 1750; the gilded copper statue of the Virgin Mary was added in 1753.

Cinephiles may recognise the central balcony of ㉓ **Palazzo Pandola**, at No 33, from the closing scene of Vittorio de Sica's *Matrimonio all'italiana* (Marriage, Italian Style), starring Sophia Loren and Marcello Mastroianni. Backtrack from the square, turning left into Via San Sebastiano. At the next intersection on your left, bookshop-lined Via Port'Alba leads down to ㉔ **Port'Alba**, a city gate built in 1625 that leads into Piazza Dante.

Double back the way you came, turn left back into Via San Sebastiano, and a block ahead on your right is ㉕ **Piazza Bellini** and its restorative cafes.

Enoteca Belledonne BAR
(✆081 40 31 62; www.enotecabelledonne.com; Vico Belledonne a Chiaia 18; ⊙10am-2pm & 4.30pm-2am Tue-Sat, 6.30pm-1am Mon & Sun; 🔊; 🚌C24 to Riviera di Chiaia) Exposed-brick walls, ambient lighting and bottle-lined shelves set a cosy scene at Chiaia's best-loved wine bar – just look for the evening crowd spilling out onto the street. Swill, sniff and eavesdrop over a list of well-chosen, mostly Italian wines, including 30 by the glass. The decent grazing menu includes charcuterie and cheese (€16), crostini (from €6) and *bruschette* (€7).

☆ Entertainment

Options run the gamut from nail-biting football games to world-class opera. For cultural listings check www.incampania. it. Tickets for most cultural events are available from ticket agency **Box Office** (✆081 551 91 88; www.boxofficenapoli.it; Galleria Umberto I 17; ⊙9.30am-8pm Mon-Fri, 9.30am-1.30pm & 4.30-8pm Sat; 🚌R2 to Piazza Trieste e Trento) or the box office inside bookshop **Feltrinelli** (✆081 032 23 62; www.azzurroservice.net; Piazza dei Martiri 23; ⊙11am-2pm & 3-8pm Mon-Sat; 🚌C24 to Piazza dei Martiri).

Teatro San Carlo OPERA, BALLET
(✆081 797 23 31; www.teatrosancarlo.it; Via San Carlo 98; ⊙box office 10am-5.30pm Mon-Sat, to 2pm Sun; 🚌R2 to Via San Carlo) One of Italy's top opera houses, the San Carlo stages opera, ballet and concerts. Bank on €50 for a place in the sixth tier, €100 for a seat in the stalls or – if you're under 30 and can prove it – €30 for a place in a side box. Ballet tickets range from €35 to €80, with €20 tickets for those under 30.

❶ Information

Loreto-Mare Hospital (Ospedale Loreto-Mare; ✆081 254 27 01, emergency 081 254 27 43; Via A Vespucci 26; 🚌154, 🚌1, 2, 4) Central-city hospital with an emergency department.
Pharmacy (Stazione Centrale; ⊙7am-9pm Mon-Sat, to 8pm Sun) Inside the train station.
Police Station (Questura; ✆081 794 11 11; Via Medina 75; Ⓜ Università) Has an office for foreigners. To report a stolen car, call ✆081 79 41 43.

TOURIST OFFICES

Head to the following tourist bureaus for information and a map of the city:

Tourist Information Office (✆081 551 27 01; Piazza del Gesù Nuovo 7; ⊙9am-5pm Mon-Sat, to 1pm Sun; Ⓜ Dante) Tourist office in the *centro storico*.
Tourist Information Office (✆081 26 87 79; Stazione Centrale; ⊙8.30am-7.30pm; Ⓜ Garibaldi) Tourist office inside Stazione Centrale (Central Station).
Tourist Information Office (✆081 40 23 94; Via San Carlo 9; ⊙9am-5pm Mon-Sat, to 1pm Sun; 🚌R2 to Via San Carlo, Ⓜ Municipio) Tourist office at Galleria Umberto I, directly opposite Teatro San Carlo.

❶ Getting There & Away

AIR

Capodichino, 7km northeast of the city centre, is southern Italy's main airport, linking Naples with most Italian and several European cities, as well as New York. Budget carrier Easyjet operates several routes to/from Capodichino, including London, Paris, Brussels and Berlin.

CAR & MOTORCYCLE

Naples is on the Autostrada del Sole, the A1 (north to Rome and Milan) and the A3 (south to Salerno and Reggio di Calabria). The A30 skirts Naples to the northeast, while the A16 heads across the Apennines to Bari.

On approaching the city, the motorways meet the Tangenziale di Napoli, a major ring road around the city. The ring road hugs the city's northern fringe, meeting the A1 for Rome in the east and continuing westwards towards the Campi Flegrei and Pozzuoli.

❶ Getting Around

TO/FROM THE AIRPORT

Airport shuttle bus Alibus connects the airport to Piazza Garibaldi (Stazione Centrale) and Molo Beverello (€3 from selected tobacconists, €4 on board; 45 minutes; every 20 minutes).

Official taxi fares from the airport are as follows: €23 to a seafront hotel or to Mergellina hydrofoil terminal, €19 to Piazza Municipio or Molo Beverello ferry terminal, and €16 to Stazione Centrale.

CAR & MOTORCYCLE

Vehicle theft, anarchic traffic and illegal parking 'attendants' make driving in Naples a bad option. Furthermore, much of the city centre is closed to nonresident traffic for much of the day.

East of the city centre, there's a 24-hour car park at Via Brin (€1.30 for the first four hours, €7.20 for 24 hours).

Ercolano & Herculaneum

Ercolano is an uninspiring Neapolitan suburb that's home to one of Italy's best-preserved ancient sites: Herculaneum. Smaller than Pompeii, Herculaneum allows you to visit without that nagging itch that you're bound to miss something.

⊙ Sights

★ **Ruins of
Herculaneum** ARCHAEOLOGICAL SITE
(☑081 732 43 27; www.pompeiisites.org; Corso Resina 187, Ercolano; adult/reduced €11/5.50, incl Pompeii €20/10; ⊙8.30am-7.30pm summer, to 5pm winter; ⋐Circumvesuviana to Ercolano-Scavi) Upstaged by its larger rival, Pompeii, Herculaneum harbours a wealth of archaeological finds. Indeed, this superbly conserved Roman fishing town of 4000 inhabitants is easier to navigate than Pompeii, and can be explored with a map and audioguide (€6.50).

From the site's main gateway on Corso Resina, head down the walkway to the ticket office (at the bottom on your left). Ticket purchased, follow the walkway to the actual entrance to the ruins (*scavi*).

Herculaneum's fate runs parallel to that of Pompeii. Destroyed by an earthquake in AD 62, the AD 79 eruption of Mt Vesuvius saw it submerged in a 16m-thick sea of mud that essentially fossilised the city. Thousands of people tried to escape by boat but were suffocated by the volcano's poisonous gases. Indeed, what appears to be a moat around the town is in fact the ancient shoreline. It was here in 1980 that archaeologists discovered some 300 skeletons, the remains of a crowd that had fled to the beach only to be overcome by the terrible heat of clouds surging down from Vesuvius.

The town itself was rediscovered in 1709 and amateur excavations were carried out intermittently until 1874, with many finds carted off to Naples to decorate the houses of the well-to-do or ending up in museums. Serious archaeological work began again in 1927 and continues to this day, although with much of the ancient site buried beneath modern Ercolano it's slow going. Indeed, note that at any given time some houses will invariably be shut for restoration.

Ruins of Herculaneum, Ercolano
MICHELE FALZONE/GETTY IMAGES ©

Terme Suburbane ARCHAEOLOGICAL SITE
(Suburban Baths; ⊙closed for restoration) Marking Herculaneum's southernmost tip is the 1st-century-AD Terme Suburbane, one of the best-preserved Roman bath complexes in existence, with deep pools, stucco friezes and bas-reliefs looking down upon marble seats and floors. This is also one of the best places to observe the soaring volcanic deposits that smothered the ancient coastline.

MAV MUSEUM
(Museo Archeologico Virtuale; ☑081 1980 6511; www.museomav.com; Via IV Novembre 44; adult/reduced €7.50/6, optional 3D documentary €4; ⊙9am-5.30pm daily Mar-Sep, reduced hours rest of the year;⋐Circumvesuviana to Ercolano-Scavi) Using high-tech holograms and computer-generated recreations, this 'virtual archaeological museum' brings ruins like Pompeii's forum and Capri's Villa Jovis back to virtual life. Especially fun for kids, it's a useful place to comprehend just how impressive those crumbling columns once were. The museum is on the main street linking Ercolano-Scavi train station to the ruins of Herculaneum.

✗ Eating

Viva Lo Re NEAPOLITAN €€
(☑081 739 02 07; www.vivalore.it; Corso Resina 261; meals €35; ⊙noon-4pm & 8.30-late Tue-Sat, noon-4pm Sun; ⋐Circumvesuviana to Ercolano-Scavi) Located 500m southeast of the ruins

of Herculaneum on Corso Resina – dubbed the Miglio d'oro (Golden Mile) for its once-glorious stretch of 18th-century villas – Viva Lo Re is a stylish osteria, where vintage prints and bookshelves meet a superb wine list, gracious staff and gorgeous, revamped regional cooking.

ℹ Information

Tourist Office (Via IV Novembre 44; ⊘ 9am-5.30pm Mon-Sat; ® Circumvesuviana to Ercolano-Scavi) Ercolano's new tourist office is located in the same building as MAV, between the Circumvesuviana Ercolano-Scavi train station and the Herculaneum ruins.

ℹ Getting There & Away

By car take the A3 from Naples, exit at Ercolano Portico and follow the signs to car parks near the site's entrance.

Mt Vesuvius

Looming over the Bay of Naples, stratovolcano **Mt Vesuvius** (☎ 081 239 56 53; adult/reduced €10/8; ⊘ 9am-6pm Jul & Aug, to 5pm Apr-Jun & Sep, to 4pm Mar & Oct, to 3pm Nov-Feb, ticket office closes 1hr before the crater) has blown its top more than 30 times. Its violent outburst in AD 79 not only drowned Pompeii in pumice and pushed the coastline back several kilometres but also destroyed much of the mountain top, creating a huge caldera and two new peaks.

What redeems this slumbering menace is the spectacular panorama from its crater, which takes in Naples, its world-famous bay, and part of the Apennine mountains.

Vesuvius itself is the focal point of the **Parco Nazionale del Vesuvio** (Vesuvius National Park; www.epnv.it), which offers nine nature walks around the volcano. A simple map of the trails can be downloaded from the park's website. Alternatively, **Naples Trips & Tours** (☎ 349 7155270; www.naplestripsandtours. com; guided tour €50) runs a daily horse-riding tour of the park (weather permitting). Running for three to four hours, the tour includes transfers to/from Naples or Ercolano-Scavi Circumvesuviana station, helmet, saddle, guide and (most importantly) coffee.

If travelling by car, exit the A3 at Ercolano Portico and follow signs for the Parco Nazionale del Vesuvio. Note that when weather conditions are bad the summit path is shut and bus departures are suspended.

Pompeii

POP 25,365

Each year about 2.5 million people pour in to wander the eerie shell of ancient Pompeii, a once thriving commercial centre. Not only an evocative glimpse into Roman life, the ruins provide a stark reminder of the malign forces that lie deep inside Mt Vesuvius.

View of Naples with Mt Vesuvius in the distance

VINTAGE VILLAS

The suburb of **Oplontis** (Via dei Sepolcri, Torre Annunziata; ⊠Circumvesuviana to Torre Annunziata) was buried beneath the streets of Torre Annunziata, and only two of its houses have been unearthed. Villa Poppaea, the only one open to the public, has outstanding, richly coloured 1st-century wall paintings in the *triclinium* (dining room) and *caldarium* (hot bathroom) in the west wing. Marking the villa's eastern border is a garden with an envy-inducing swimming pool (17m by 61m).

South of Oplontis, **Stabiae** (Via Passeggiata Archeologica, Castellammare di Stabia; ⊠Circumvesuviana to Via Nocera) stood on the slopes of the Varano hill overlooking what was then the sea and is now modern Castellammare di Stabia. You can visit two villas: the 1st-century-BC Villa Arianna and the larger Villa San Marco. Neither is in mint condition, but the frescoes in Villa Arianna suggest that it must once have been quite something.

Some 3km north of Pompeii, the archaeological site of **Boscoreale** (Via Settetermini, Boscoreale; ⊠Circumvesuviana to Pompeii-Scavi-Villa dei Misteri) consists of a rustic country villa dating back to the 1st century BC, and a fascinating antiquarium showcasing artefacts from the surrounding region. Among the more unusual items on display are shreds of Roman fabric, eggshells from Pompeii and a carbonised loaf of bread. Closed for restoration on our last visit, the villa was due to reopen sometime in mid-2016; check www.pompeiisites.org or contact the Pompeii tourist office for updates.

Opening times across the sites are standard: 8.30am to 7.30pm (last entry 6pm) April to October, 8.30am to 5pm (last entry 3.30pm) November to March. All three sites are covered by a single ticket (adult/reduced €5.50/2.75). The sites are also covered by a five-sites cumulative ticket (adult/reduced €20/10), which also includes Pompeii and Herculaneum.

⊙ Sights

★ **Ruins of Pompeii** ARCHAEOLOGICAL SITE
(⌨ 081 857 53 47; www.pompeiisites.org; entrances at Porta Marina, Piazza Esedra & Piazza Anfiteatro; adult/reduced €11/5.50, incl Herculaneum €20/10; ⊙8.30am-7.30pm summer, to 5pm winter) The ghostly ruins of ancient Pompeii (Pompei in Italian) make for one of the world's most engrossing archaeological experiences. Much of the site's value lies in the fact that the town wasn't simply blown away by Vesuvius in AD 79 but buried under a layer of *lapilli* (burning fragments of pumice stone). The result is a remarkably well-preserved slice of ancient life, where visitors can walk down Roman streets and snoop around millennia-old houses, temples, shops, cafes, amphitheatres, and even a brothel.

The origins of Pompeii are uncertain, but it seems likely that it was founded in the 7th century BC by the Campanian Oscans. Over the next seven centuries the city fell to the Greeks and the Samnites before becoming a Roman colony in 80 BC.

In AD 62, a mere 17 years before Vesuvius erupted, the city was struck by a major earthquake. Damage was widespread and much of the city's 20,000-strong population was evacuated. Fortunately, many had not returned by the time Vesuvius blew, but 2000 men, women and children perished nevertheless.

After its catastrophic demise, Pompeii receded from the public eye until 1594, when the architect Domenico Fontana stumbled across the ruins while digging a canal. Exploration proper, however, didn't begin until 1748.

In recent years, the site has suffered a number of high-profile incidents due to bad weather. Most recently, heavy rain caused the wall of an ancient shop to collapse in March 2014. Maintenance work is ongoing, but progress is beset by political, financial and bureaucratic problems.

➡ **Terme Suburbane**

Just outside ancient Pompeii's city walls, this 1st-century-BC bathhouse is famous for several erotic frescoes that scandalised the Vatican when they were revealed in 2001. The panels decorate what was once the *apodyterium* (changing room). The room leading to the colourfully frescoed *frigidarium* (cold-water bath) features fragments of stuccowork, as well as one of the few original roofs to survive at Pompeii. Beyond the *tepadarium* (tepid bath) and *caldarium* (hot bath) rooms are the remains of a heated outdoor swimming pool.

Tragedy in Pompeii

24 AUGUST AD 79

8am Buildings including the **Terme Suburbane ❶** and the **foro ❷** are still undergoing repair after an earthquake in AD 63 caused significant damage to the city. Despite violent earth tremors overnight, residents have little idea of the catastrophe that lies ahead.

Midday Peckish locals pour into the **Thermopolium di Vetutius Placidus ❸**. The lustful slip into the **Lupanare ❹**, and gladiators practise for the evening's planned games at the **anfiteatro ❺**. A massive boom heralds the eruption. Shocked onlookers witness a dark cloud of volcanic matter shoot some 14km above the crater.

3pm–5pm Lapilli (burning pumice stone) rains down on Pompeii. Terrified locals begin to flee; others take shelter. Within two hours, the plume is 25km high and the sky has darkened. Roofs collapse under the weight of the debris, burying those inside.

25 AUGUST AD 79

Midnight Mudflows bury the town of Herculaneum. Lapilli and ash continue to rain down on Pompeii, bursting through buildings and suffocating those taking refuge within.

4am–8am Ash and gas avalanches hit Herculaneum. Subsequent surges smother Pompeii, killing all remaining residents, including those in the **Orto dei Fuggiaschi ❻**. The volcanic 'blanket' will safeguard frescoed treasures like the **Casa del Menandro ❼** and **Villa dei Misteri ❽** for almost two millennia.

TOP TIPS

» Visit in the afternoon
» Allow three hours
» Wear comfortable shoes and a hat
» Bring drinking water
» Don't use flash photography

Terme Suburbane
The *laconicum* (sauna), *caldarium* (hot bath) and large, heated swimming pool weren't the only sources of heat here; scan the walls of this suburban bathhouse for some of the city's raunchiest frescoes.

Villa di Diomede

Casa del Poeta Tragico

Porta Ercolano

Casa del Fauno

Basilica

Tempio di Apollo

Porta Marina ❶

Terme del Foro

❷

❹

Macellum

Teatro Grande

Quadriportico dei Teatri

Porta di Stabia

Teatro Piccolo

Foro
An ancient Times Square of sorts, the forum sits at the intersection of Pompeii's main streets and was closed to traffic in the 1st century AD. The plinths on the southern edge featured statues of the imperial family.

CRISTIAN BONETTO ©

Villa dei Misteri
Home to the world-famous *Dionysiac Frieze* fresco. Other highlights at this villa include *trompe l'oeil* wall decorations in the *cubiculum* (bedroom) and Egyptian-themed artwork in the *tablinum* (reception).

Lupanare
The prostitutes at this brothel were often slaves of Greek or Asian origin. Mattresses once covered the stone beds and the names engraved in the walls are possibly those of the workers and their clients.

Thermopolium di Vetutius Placidus
The counter at this ancient snack bar once held urns filled with hot food. The *lararium* (house-hold shrine) on the back wall depicts Dionysus (the god of wine) and Mercury (the god of profit and commerce).

Casa dei Vettii

Porta del Vesuvio

EYEWITNESS ACCOUNT

Pliny the Younger (AD 61–c 112) gives a gripping, first-hand account of the catastrophe in his letters to Tacitus (AD 56–117).

Porta di Nola

Casa della Venere in Conchiglia

Porta di Sarno

③

⑦

⑥

Grande Palestra

⑤

Tempio di Iside

Orto dei Fuggiaschi
The Garden of the Fugitives showcases the plaster moulds of 13 locals seeking refuge during Vesuvius' eruption – the largest number of victims found in any one area. The huddled bodies make for a moving scene.

Anfiteatro
Magistrates, local senators and the games' sponsors and organisers enjoyed front-row seating at this veteran amphitheatre, home to gladiatorial battles and the odd riot. The parapet circling the stadium featured paintings of combat, victory celebrations and hunting scenes.

Casa del Menandro
This dwelling most likely belonged to the family of Poppaea Sabina, Nero's second wife. A room to the left of the atrium features Trojan War paintings and a polychrome mosaic of pygmies rowing down the Nile.

Old Pompeii

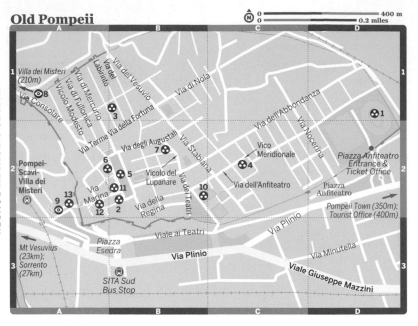

Old Pompeii

➡ Porta Marina

The ruins of Pompeii's main entrance is at Porta Marina, the most impressive of the seven gates that punctuated the ancient town walls. A busy passageway now, as it was then, it originally connected the town with the nearby harbour, hence the gateway's name. Immediately on the right as you enter the gate is the 1st-century-BC **Tempio di Venere** (Temple of Venus), formerly one of the town's most opulent temples.

➡ Foro

(Forum) A huge grassy rectangle flanked by limestone columns, the *foro* was ancient Pompeii's main piazza, as well as the site of gladiatorial battles before the Anfiteatro was constructed. The buildings surrounding the forum are testament to its role as the city's hub of commercial, political and religious activity.

➡ Basilica

The basilica was the 2nd-century-BC seat of Pompeii's law courts and exchange. Their semicircular apses would later influence the design of early Christian churches.

➡ Tempio di Apollo

(Temple of Apollo) The oldest and most important of Pompeii's religious buildings, the Tempio di Apollo largely dates to the 2nd century BC, including the striking columned portico. Fragments remain of an earlier version dating to the 6th century BC.

➡ Granai del Foro

(Forum Granary) The Granai del Foro is used to store hundreds of amphorae and a number of body casts that were made in the late 19th century by pouring plaster into the hollows left by disintegrated bodies. Among these casts is a pregnant slave; the belt around her waist would have displayed the name of her owner.

➡ Lupanare

Ancient Pompeii's only dedicated brothel, Lupanare is a tiny two-storey building with five rooms on each floor. Its collection of raunchy frescoes was a menu of sorts for clients. The walls in the rooms are carved with graffiti – including declarations of love and hope written by the brothel workers – in various languages.

➡ Teatro Grande

The 2nd-century-BC Teatro Grande was a huge 5000-seat theatre carved into the lava mass on which Pompeii was originally built.

➡ Casa del Menandro

Better preserved than the larger Casa del Fauno, luxurious Casa del Menandro has an outstanding, elegant peristyle (a colonnade-framed courtyard) beyond its beautifully frescoed atrium. On the peristyle's far right side a doorway leads to a private bathhouse, lavished with exquisite frescoes and mosaics. The central room off the far end of the peristyle features a striking mosaic of the ancient Greek dramatist Menander, after which the rediscovered villa was named.

➡ Anfiteatro

(Amphitheatre) Gladiatorial battles thrilled up to 20,000 spectators at the grassy *anfiteatro*. Built in 70 BC, it's the oldest known Roman amphitheatre in existence.

➡ Casa del Fauno

(House of the Faun) Covering an entire *insula* (city block) and boasting two atria at its front end (humbler homes had one), Pompeii's largest private house is named after the delicate bronze statue in the *impluvium* (rain tank). It was here that early excavators found Pompeii's greatest mosaics, most of which are now in Naples' Museo Archeologico Nazionale (p55). Valuable on-site survivors include a beautiful, geometrically patterned marble floor.

Villa dei Misteri ARCHAEOLOGICAL SITE

This recently restored, 90-room villa is one of the most complete structures left standing in Pompeii. The dionysiac frieze, the most important fresco still on site, spans the walls of the large dining room. One of the biggest and most arresting paintings from the ancient world, it depicts the initiation of a bride-to-be into the cult of Dionysus, the Greek god of wine. A farm for much of its life, the villa's *vino*-making area is still visible at the northern end. Follow Via Consolare out of the town through **Porta Ercolano**. Continue past **Villa di Diomede**, turn right, and you'll come to Villa dei Misteri.

🛏 Sleeping & Eating

The ruins are best visited on a day trip from Naples, Sorrento or Salerno; once the excavations close for the day, the area around the site becomes decidedly seedy. Most of the restaurants near the ruins are characterless affairs set up for feeding busloads of tourists. Down in the modern town are a few decent restaurants serving excellent local food.

If you'd rather eat at the ruins, the on-site cafeteria peddles the standard choice of *panini*, pizza slices, salads, and gelato.

⭐**President** CAMPANIAN €€

(📋081 850 72 45; www.ristorantepresident.it; Piazza Schettini 12; meals €35; ⊘noon-4pm & 7pm-midnight, closed Mon Oct-Apr; 🚇FS to Pompei, 🚇Circumvesuviana to Pompei Scavi-Villa dei Misteri') With its dripping chandeliers and gracious service, the Michelin-starred President feels like a private dining room in an Audrey Hepburn film. At the helm is charming owner-chef Paolo Gramaglia, whose passion for local produce, history and culinary creativity translates into bread made to ancient Roman recipes, slow-cooked snapper paired with tomato puree and sweet-onion gelato, and deconstructed *pastiera* (sweet Neapolitan tart).

ℹ Information

Tourist Office (📋081 850 72 55; Via Sacra 1; ⊘8.30am-3.30pm Mon-Fri) Located in the centre of the modern town.

ℹ Getting There & Away

To get here by car, take the A3 from Naples. Use the Pompeii exit and follow signs to Pompeii Scavi. Car parks (approximately €5 per hour) are clearly marked and vigorously touted.

ℹ TOURS

You'll almost certainly be approached by a guide outside the *scavi* (excavations) ticket office: note that authorised guides wear identification tags. If considering a guided tour of the ruins, reputable tour operators include **Yellow Sudmarine** (📋329 1010328, 334 1047036; www.yellowsudmarine.com; 2hr Pompeii guided tour €110) and **Walks of Italy** (www.walksofitaly.com; 2½hr Pompeii guided tour €52), both of which also offer excursions to other areas of Campania.

Sorrento makes a good base for exploring the region's highlights: to the south is the best of the peninsula's unspoilt countryside, to the east is the Amalfi Coast, to the north lie Pompeii and other archaeological sites, and offshore is the fabled island of Capri.

Sorrento & Around

SORRENTO

POP 16,500

Despite being a popular package-holiday destination, Sorrento manages to retain a laid-back southern-Italian charm. There are very few sights to speak of, but there are wonderful views of Mt Vesuvius, and its small *centro storico* is an atmospheric place to explore. The main drawback is the lack of a proper beach: the town straddles the cliffs overlooking the water to Naples.

◉ Sights

Museo Correale   MUSEUM
(☑ 081 878 18 46; www.museocorreale.it; Via Correale 50; admission €7; ◷ 9.30am-6.30pm Tue-Sat, to 1.30pm Sun) East of the city centre, this museum is well worth a visit whether you're a clock collector, an archaeological egghead

or into embroidery. In addition to the rich assortment of 17th- to 19th-century Neapolitan art and crafts, there are Japanese, Chinese and European ceramics, clocks, furniture and, on the ground floor, Greek and Roman artefacts. The bulk of the collection, along with the 18th-century villa housing it, was donated to the city in the 1920s by aristocratic counts Alfredo and Pompeo Correale. Be sure to wander around the gardens, with their breathtaking coastal views and rare plants and flowers.

Marina Grande   HARBOUR
(Via Marina Grande) The closest thing to a *spiaggia* (beach) is this pleasant sandy stretch at Marina Grande harbour; if you want to just loll in the sun, nearby jetties sport umbrellas and deckchairs. While it's far smaller than the island of Procida in the Bay of Naples, this former fishing district has a glimmer of similarity, with its pastel-coloured houses, brightly painted boats and fishermen mending nets. There are some earthy seafood restaurants serving fish from the morning's catch.

Sedile Dominava   HISTORIC BUILDING
(Via San Cesareo) Incongruously wedged between racks of lemon-themed souvenir merchandise, this 15th-century domed *palazzo* (mansion) has exquisite, albeit faded, original frescoes. Crowned by a cupola, the terrace was originally a meeting point for the town's medieval aristocracy; today it houses a working men's club where local pensioners sit around playing cards.

PLAN YOUR ROUTE
••••••••••••••••••••••••••••••••••••••

1 **Amalfi Coast** (p17) Starting in Vico Equense, this trip passes through Sorrento to the west tip of the coast, visiting green hilltop towns Sant'Agata sui due Golfi and Marina del Cantone.

3 **Southern Larder** (p37) With an optional jaunt to Capri, this trip starts in Sorrento and heads north to Vico Equense before meeting back up with the Amalfi coast.

Centro Storico AREA

(Corso Italia) The bustling *centro storico* (historic centre) ranges along Corso Italia, a major hub for shops, restaurants and bars. Duck into the side streets and you'll find narrow lanes flanked by traditional green-shuttered buildings, interspersed with the occasional *palazzo,* piazza or church. Souvenir shops, trattorias and some fine old buildings also jostle for space in this tangle of cobbled backstreets.

Duomo CATHEDRAL

(Corso Italia; ⊙ 8am-12.30pm & 4.30-9pm) To get a feel for Sorrento's history, stroll down Via Pietà from Piazza Tasso and past two medieval palaces en route to the cathedral, with its striking exterior fresco, triple-tiered bell tower, four classical columns and elegant majolica clock. Take note of the striking marble bishop's throne (1573) and the beautiful wooden choir stalls decorated in the local *intarsio* style. The cathedral's original structure dates from the 15th century, but the building has been altered several times, most recently in the early 20th century when the current facade was added.

Museo Bottega della Tarsia Lignea MUSEUM

(☑ 081 877 19 42; www.museomuta.it; Via San Nicola 28; adult/reduced €8/5; ⊙ 10am-6.30pm Apr-Oct, to 5pm Nov-Mar) Since the 18th century, Sorrento has been famous for its *intarsio* furniture, made with elaborately designed inlaid wood. Some wonderful examples can be found in this museum, housed in an 18th-century palace, complete with beautiful frescoes. There's also an interesting collection of paintings, prints and photographs depicting the town and surrounding area in the 19th century. If you're interested in purchasing a new *intarsio* piece, visit Gargiulo & Jannuzzi (p78), one of the longest-established specialist shops in town; they are happy to ship purchases.

Chiesa di San Francesco CHURCH

(Via San Francesco; ⊙ 8am-1pm & 2-8pm) Located next to the Villa Comunale Park, this is one of Sorrento's most beautiful churches. Surrounded by bougainvillea and birdsong, the evocative cloisters have an Arabic portico and interlaced arches supported by octagonal pillars. The church is most famous, however, for its summer program of concerts featuring world-class performers from the classical school. If this strikes a chord, check out the schedule at the tourist office. There are also regular art exhibitions.

Il Vallone dei Mulino HISTORIC SITE

(Valley of the Mills; Via Fuorimura) 🌿 Just behind Piazza Tasso, a stunning natural phenomenon is on view from Via Fuorimura. Il Vallone dei Mulino is a deep mountain cleft that dates from a volcanic eruption 35,000 years ago. Sorrento was once bounded by three gorges, but today this is the only one that remains. The valley is named after the ancient wheat mills that were once located here, the ruins of which are still clearly visible.

🏃 Activities

★ Sic Sic BOATING

(☑ 081 807 22 83; www.nauticasicsic.com; Marina Piccola; ⊙ May-Oct) Seek out the best beaches by rented boat, with or without a skipper. This outfit rents a variety of motor boats, starting at around €40 per hour or €100 per day. It also organises boat excursions, wedding shoots and similar.

Bagni Regina Giovanna SWIMMING

Sorrento lacks a decent beach, so consider heading to Bagni Regina Giovanna, a rocky beach with clear, clean water about 2km west of town, set among the ruins of the Roman Villa Pollio Felix. It's possible to walk here (follow Via Capo), although you'll save your strength if you get the SITA bus headed for Massa Lubrense.

Villa Comunale Park OUTDOORS

(⊙ 8am-midnight summer, to 10.30pm winter) This landscaped park commands stunning views across the water to Mt Vesuvius. A popular green space to while away the sunset hours, it's a lively spot, with benches, operatic buskers and a small bar.

🎓 Courses

Sorrento Cooking School COOKING COURSE

(☑ 081 878 35 55; www.sorrentocookingschool.com; Viale dei Pini 52, Sant'Agnello; ⊙ Apr-Oct) You can opt for a serious culinary vacation here or one of the popular three-hour classes (€60), learning to make such Italian staples as pizza, ravioli and tiramisu (OK, more a sin than a staple)

> ## BEST AMALFI COAST BEACHES
> ....
> **Baia de Ieranto** (p82)
>
> **Spiaggia di Fornillo** (p90)
>
> **Marina di Praia** (p91)
>
> **Bagni Regina Giovanna**

Sorrento

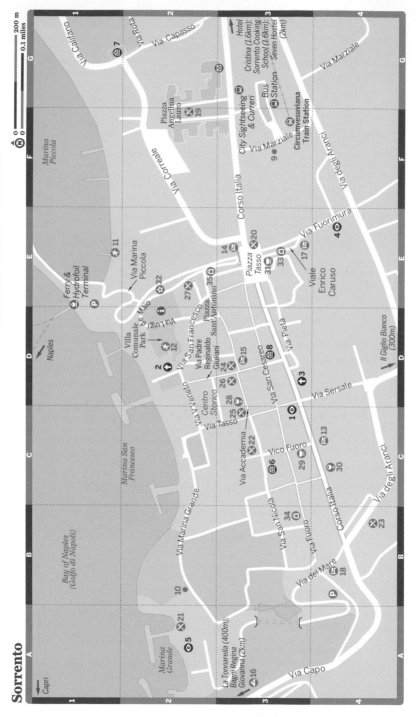

Sorrento

in a beautiful spot surrounded by lemon trees. The class ends with a meal of the goodies prepared, accompanied by local wine.

Sant'Anna Institute   LANGUAGE COURSE
(Sorrento Lingue; ☎ 081 807 55 99; www.sorrentolingue.com; Via Marina Gra nde 16) There is something very appealing about rattling off your shopping list in faultless Italian. This is one of the longest-establ ished language schools on the Amalfi Coast, attracting students from all over the globe. Prices start at €198 for a week of tuition, plus a €60 enrolment fee. It also runs language/cooking and language/history courses.

★☆ Festivals & Events

Sant'Antonino   RELIGIOUS
(⊙14 Feb) The city's patron saint, Sant'-Antonino, is remembered annually with processions and huge markets. The saint is credited with having saved Sorrento during WWII when Salerno and Naples were heavily bombed.

Settimana Santa   RELIGIOUS
(Holy Week) Famed throughout Italy; the first procession takes place at midnight on the Thursday preceding Good Friday, with robed and hooded penitents in white; the second occurs on Good Friday, when participants wear black robes and hoods to commemorate the death of Christ.

Sagra della Salsiccia e Ceppone   FOOD
(⊙13 Dec) Sausage lovers can salivate at this annual festival, when hundreds of kilos of sausages are barbecued over a giant bonfire, accompanied by hearty local wine.

🛏 Sleeping

★Ulisse   HOSTEL €
(☎081 877 47 53; www.ulissedeluxe.com; Via del Mare 22; dm €30, d €60-120; P ❄ 🛜) Although it calls itself a hostel, the Ulisse is about as far from a backpackers' pad as a hiking boot from a stiletto. Most rooms are plush, spacious affairs with swish if rather bland fabrics, gleaming floors and large en-suite bathrooms. There are two single-sex dorms, and quads for sharers. Breakfast is included in some rates but costs €10 with others.

Facilities include an adjacent Wellness Centre where guests can use the pool for just €5 and enjoy free fitness sessions and reasonably priced treatments.

Casa Astarita   B&B €
(☎081 877 49 06; www.casastarita.com; Corso Italia 67; d €90-130, tr €110-150; ❄ 🛜) Housed in a 16th-century *palazzo* on Sorrento's main strip, this charming B&B has a colourful, eclectic look with original vaulted ceilings, brightly painted doors and majolica-tiled floors. Its six simple but well-equipped rooms surround a central parlour, where breakfast is served on a large rustic table.

Seven Hostel
HOSTEL €

(☏ 081 878 67 58; www.sevenhostel.com; Via Iommella Grande 99, Sant'Agnello; dm/d from €15/50; ⊘ year-round; ❄ @ 🔊) The ethos of the owners here is to offer the best hostel in the world, and the first *ostello di design*. Located in an 8th-century former convent surrounded by olive and lemon trees, the hostel has chic rooftop terraces with decking and loungers, weekend live music and the more down-to-earth perk of an on-site laundry. Rooms are contemporary and spacious.

Nube d'Argento
CAMPGROUND €

(☏ 081 878 13 44; www.nubedargento.com; Via Capo 21; camping per 2 people, car & tent €38, 2-person bungalows €60-85, 4-person bungalows €90-120; ⊘ Mar-Dec; @ 🏊) This inviting campground is an easy 1km drive west of the Sorrento city centre. Pitches and wooden chalet-style bungalows are spread out beneath a canopy of olive trees – a source of much-needed summer shade – and the facilities are excellent. Kids in particular will enjoy the open-air swimming pool, table-tennis table, slides and swings.

★ Hotel Cristina
HOTEL €€

(☏ 081 878 35 62; www.hotelcristinasorrento. it; Via Privata Rubinacci 6, Sant'Agnello; s/d/tr/q €130/150/180/200; ⊘ Mar-Oct; ❄ 🔊 🏊) Located

---

---

high above Sant'Agnello, this hotel has superb views, particularly from the swimming pool. The spacious rooms have sea-view balconies and combine inlaid wooden furniture with contemporary flourishes like Philippe Starck chairs. There's an in-house restaurant and a free shuttle bus to/from Sorrento's Circumvesuviana train station.

Hotel Astoria
HOTEL €€

(☏ 081 807 40 30; www.hotelastoriasorrento.com; Via Santa Maria delle Grazie 24; s €50-110, €70-170; ❄ 🔊) This renovated classic has the advantage of being located in the heart of the *centro storico*. Overall, it's an excellent choice. The interior sparkles with colourful glossy tiles and blue and buttercup-yellow paintwork. The large enclosed back terrace is a delight, with seats set under orange and lemon trees and colourful tiled murals lining the back wall.

La Tonnarella
HOTEL €€

(☏ 081 878 11 53; www.latonnarella.com; Via Capo 31; d €120-140, ste €240-350; ⊘ Apr-Oct & Christmas; P ❄ @ 🔊) A splendid choice (but not for minimalists), La Tonnarella is a dazzling canvas of majolica tiles, antiques, chandeliers and statues. Rooms, most with their own balcony or small terrace, continue the sumptuous classical theme with traditional furniture and discreet mod cons. The hotel also has its own private beach, accessible by lift, and a highly regarded terrace restaurant.

★ Grand Hotel Excelsior Vittoria
HOTEL €€€

(☏ 081 807 10 44; www.exvitt.it; Piazza Tasso 34; s/d/ste from €350/400/700; P ❄ 🔊 🏊) A hotel for over 170 years, the grand old dame of Sorrento oozes belle époque elegance. Huge potted palms adorn gilded public rooms awash with antique furniture. Rooms vary in size and style, ranging from tasteful simplicity to extravagant, frescoed opulence, but all have views either of the hotel's gardens dripping with crimson bougainvillea or over the sea to Vesuvius. Past guests have included Pavarotti, Wagner, Goethe, Sophia Loren and British royalty.

Plaza Hotel
HOTEL €€€

(☏ 081 878 28 31; www.plazasorrento.com; Via Fuorimura 3; d from €220; P ❄ @ 🔊) This is one of the newer hotels in town: the whole place sports a bright, contemporary look with dazzling white contrasting with earthy parquet floors, accented by splashes of colour. Abstracts adorn the walls, and the rooftop sky

Gelati on display

bar (round the corner from the infinity pool) is perfect for a sundowner, with its scenic views of town and sea.

✕ Eating

★ Da Emilia
TRATTORIA €

(☑ 081 807 27 20; Via Marina Grande 62; meals €20; ☉ noon-2.30pm & 7pm-midnight; ♠) Founded in 1947 and still run by the same family, this is a homely yet atmospheric joint overlooking the fishing boats in Marina Grande. There's a large informal dining room, complete with youthful photos of former patron Sophia Loren, a scruffily romantic terrace and a menu of straightforward, no-fail dishes like mussels with lemon, and spaghetti with clams.

Angelina Lauro
ITALIAN €

(☑ 081 807 40 97; Piazza Angelina Lauro 39-40; self-service meals €15; ☉ 10am-11pm Wed-Mon; ♠) Rafael is your congenial host at this brightly lit, roomy place that has a passing resemblance to a college canteen and has been family run since 1980. It hits the spot for a filling, inexpensive self-service lunch: grab a tray and choose from the selection of pastas, meats and vegetable side dishes. The owners produce their own wine and olive oil.

★ L'Antica Trattoria
ITALIAN €€

(☑ 081 807 10 82; www.lanticatrattoria.com; Via Padre Reginaldo Giuliani 33; mains €21-25, 4 courses €60; ☉ noon-11pm) Head to the upstairs terrace with its traditional tiles and trailing grape vines and you seem miles away from the alleyways outside. With a deserved reputation as the finest restaurant in town, it has a mainly traditional menu, with home-made pasta and a daily fish special. There are vegetarian and gluten-free menus, plus a resident mandolin player.

Aurora Light
ITALIAN €€

(☑ 081 877 26 31; www.auroralight.it; Piazza Tasso 3-4; mains €15; ☉ noon-midnight) At first glance the menu here looks more Californian than Campanian, with such imaginative salads as spicy chickpea and spinach, and fennel with beetroot and orange. The enthusiastic young owner has tapped into traditional dishes and given them an innovative twist: white-bean soup with baby squid, aubergine *parmigiana* with swordfish sauce, stuffed-pepper roulade and so on. The setting on Piazza Tasso is one of the best for people-watching, though one of the worst for exhaust fumes.

Inn Bufalito
ITALIAN €€

(☑ 081 365 69 75; www.innbufalito.it; Vico Fuoro 21; meals €25; ☉ 11am-midnight; ☏ ♪) ❤ Owner Franco Coppola (no relation to the movie man) exudes a real passion for showcasing local produce – the restaurant is a member of the Slow Food movement. A mozzarella bar as well as a restaurant, this effortlessly stylish place boasts a menu including delights such as Sorrento-style cheese fondue and buffalo-meat *carpaccio*. Cheese tastings are a regular event, along with photography and art exhibitions, and occasional live music.

O'Murzill
NEAPOLITAN €€

(☑081 020 23 71; Via Accademia 17; meals from €20; ⊙11.30am-1.30am Mon-Sat) With just six gingham-clothed tables in what resembles a homey front room with the kitchen beyond, this restaurant looks as though it belongs in a small village rather than in the heart of Sorrento. The reassuringly brief menu concentrates on traditional Neapolitan dishes like pasta with lobster and no-fuss antipasti such as grilled mushrooms.

There's no complimentary *limoncello* (lemon liqueur) or tomato-topped bruschetta, just well-priced and honest home-style cooking.

Refood
ITALIAN €€

(☑081 878 14 80; www.refoods.it; Via Accademia 10; meals €35; ⊙5.30pm-midnight) The postmodern decor, with its imaginative lighting and exposed steel pipes, is a far cry from that of Sorrento's traditional trattorias. Go for one of the specialities like large tube pasta in a fish stew or a classic Châteaubriand.

La Fenice
ITALIAN €€

(☑081 878 16 52; www.ristorantelafenicesorrento.com; Via degli Aranci 11; meals €24; ⊙noon-2.45pm & 7-11.30pm Tue-Sun) It's too large and bright for a romantic dinner for two, but locals continue to recommend this place for its down-to-earth, well-prepared dishes, particularly the seafood, such as mussels with garlic and parsley, and grilled squid.

Ristorante il Buco
ITALIAN €€€

(☑081 878 23 54; www.ilbucoristorante.it; Rampa Marina Piccola 5; meals €60; ⊙12.30-2.30pm & 7.30-11pm Thu-Tue Feb-Dec) Housed in a former monks' wine cellar, this dress-up restaurant offers far-from-monastic cuisine. The emphasis is on innovative regional cooking, so expect modern combos such as pasta with rockfish sauce, or *treccia* (local cheese) and prawns served on capers with tomato and olive sauce. In summer there's outdoor seating near one of the city's ancient gates. Reservations recommended.

🍸 Drinking & Nightlife

Cafè Latino
CAFE, BAR

(☑081 878 37 18; Vico Fuoro 4a; ⊙10am-1am summer) Think locked-eyes-over-cocktails time. This is the place to impress your date with cocktails (from €7) on the terrace, surrounded by orange and lemon trees. Sip a Mary Pickford (rum, pineapple, *grenadino* and maraschino) or a glass of chilled white wine.

If you can't drag yourselves away, you can also eat here (meals around €30).

Bollicine
WINE BAR

(☑081 878 46 16; Via Accademia 9; ⊙7.30pm-2am) The wine list at this unpretentious bar with a dark, woody interior includes all the big Italian names and a selection of interesting local labels. If you can't decide what to go for, the amiable bar staff will advise you. There's also a small menu of *panini* (sandwiches), bruschettas and one or two pasta dishes.

English Inn
PUB

(☑081 807 43 57; www.englishinn.it; Corso Italia 55; ⊙9am-2am) The vast upstairs garden terrace, with its orange trees and dazzle of bougainvillea, is a delight and attracts a primarily expat crowd, who head here for the disco beats and karaoke nights, accompanied by Guinness on tap. The party atmosphere continues late into the night, while the bacon-and-eggs breakfast is a suitable reviver.

Fauno Bar
CAFE

(☑081 878 11 35; Piazza Tasso; ⊙7am-midnight mid-Mar–mid-Jan) On Piazza Tasso, this elegant cafe with besuited waiters covers half the square and offers the best people-watching in town. It serves stiff drinks at stiff prices: cocktails start around €8.50. Snacks and sandwiches are also available (from €7).

☆ Entertainment

Teatro Tasso
THEATRE

(☑081 807 55 25; www.teatrotasso.it; Piazza Sant'Antonino; admission incl cocktail €25; ⊙Sorrento Musical 9.30pm summer) The southern-Italian equivalent of a London old-time music hall, Teatro Tasso is home to the *Sorrento Musical,* a sentimental 75-minute revue of Neapolitan classics such as 'O Sole Mio' and 'Trona a Sorrent'.

🛍 Shopping

Gargiulo & Jannuzzi
ARTS, CRAFTS

(☑081 878 10 41; www.gargiulo-jannuzzi.it; Viale Enrico Caruso 1; ⊙8am-8pm May-Oct, 9am-7pm Nov, Dec, Mar & Apr) Dating from 1863, this old-fashioned warehouse-shop is a classic. Knowledgable assistants guide you through the three floors of locally made goods, ranging from ceramic crockery to *intarsio* wooden pieces, embroidered lace and pottery. The prices are as good as you will get anywhere in town and the choice is certainly superior. Shipping is free for purchases over €220.

La Rapida

SHOES

(📞 338 877705; Via Fuoro 67; ⊘ 9am-8pm) There are numerous shops selling leather sandals in the *centro storico*, but head to the far end of Via Fuoro and you'll find this tiny cobbler. An old-fashioned shop, it doesn't have a huge range, but the quality's as good as anywhere else and the prices (from €30) are generally better. It also does repairs.

Stinga

ARTS, CRAFTS

(📞 081 878 11 30; www.stingatarsia.com; Via Luigi de Maio 16; ⊘ 9am-8.30pm) Well worth seeking out, this place sells distinctive inlaid-wood items made in Sorrento by the same family of craftsmen (and women) for three generations. The pieces are highly original, especially in their use of colour and design, which is often mosaic or geometric. Fine jewellery, including coral pieces, is also on display, made by family member Amulè.

ℹ️ Information

Main Tourist Office (📞 081 807 40 33; www. sorrentotourism.com; Via Luigi de Maio 35; ⊘ 8.30am-8pm Mon-Sat, 9am-1pm Sun Jul-Sep) In the Circolo dei Forestieri (Foreigners' Club). Ask for the useful publication *Surrentum*.

ℹ️ Getting There & Away

CAR & MOTORCYCLE

Coming from Naples and the north, take the A3 autostrada until Castellammare di Stabia; exit there and follow the SS145 south.

ℹ️ Getting Around

TO/FROM THE AIRPORT

Naples' Capodichino Airport is the closest airport to Sorrento and the Amalfi Coast.

Taxi

A taxi from the airport to Sorrento costs €85.

CAR & MOTORCYCLE

Autoservizi De Martino (📞 081 878 28 01; www.autoservizidemartino.com; Via Parsano 8) Has cars from €54 a day and €280 per week, plus 50cc scooters from €23 for four hours.

Avis (📞 081 878 24 59; www.avisautonoleggio. it; Corso Italia 322)

Hertz (📞 081 807 16 46; www.hertz.it; Via Capo 8)

Parking

In midsummer finding a parking spot can be a frustrating business, particularly as much of the parking on the side streets is for residents only and the city centre is closed to traffic for most of the day. There are well-signposted car parks near the ferry terminal, on the corner of Via degli Aranci and Via Renato, and heading west out of town near Via Capo (€2 per hour).

WEST OF SORRENTO

If you are here in midsummer, consider escaping the crowds by heading to the green hills around Sorrento. Known as the land of the sirens, in honour of the mythical maiden-monsters who were said to live on Li Galli (a tiny archipelago off the peninsula's southern coast), the area to the west of Massa Lubrense is among the least developed and most beautiful in the country.

Tortuous roads wind their way through hills covered in olive trees and lemon groves, passing through sleepy villages and tiny fishing ports. There are magnificent views at every turn, the best from the high points overlooking Punta Campanella, the westernmost point of the Sorrento Peninsula. Offshore, Capri looks tantalisingly close.

HIKING THE PENINSULA

Forming a giant horseshoe between **Punta Campanella** and **Punta Penna**, the beautiful **Baia di Ieranto** is generally regarded as the top swimming spot on the Sorrento Peninsula. To get there you have two alternatives: get a boat, or walk from the village of Nerano, the steep descent forming part of a longer 6.5km hike from nearby Termini.

This picturesque path is just one of 20 (for a total of 110km) that cover the area. These range from tough all-day treks such as the 14.1km **Alta Via dei Monti Lattari** from the Fontanelle hills near Positano down to the Punta Campanella, to shorter walks suitable for all the family.

Tourist offices throughout the area can provide maps detailing the colour-coded routes. With the exception of the Alta Via dei Monti Lattari, which is marked in red and white, long routes are shown in red on the map; coast-to-coast trails in blue; paths connecting villages in green; and circular routes in yellow. On the ground, trails are fairly well marked, although you may find that some signs have faded to near-indecipherable levels.

Massa Lubrense
FRANCO BANFI/GETTY IMAGES ©

Massa Lubrense

The first town you come to following the coast west from Sorrento is Massa Lubrense. Situated 120m above sea level, it's a disjointed place, comprising a small town centre and 17 *frazioni* (fractions or hamlets) joined by an intricate network of paths and mule tracks.

◎ Sights & Activities

Chiesa di Santa Maria della Grazia CHURCH
(Largo Vescovado; ⊙ 7am-noon & 4.30-8pm) The town's former cathedral, the 16th-century Chiesa di Santa Maria della Grazia, is worth a quick look for its bright majolica-tiled floor, which would look *so* good in your kitchen back home. The church stands on the northern flank of the central Largo Vescovado. Don't forget your camera, as there are fabulous views over Capri from here.

Marina della Lobra HARBOUR
From central Largo Vescovado it's a 2km descent to this pretty little marina backed by ramshackle houses and verdant slopes – or, rather, it's a 40-minute downhill walk and a wheezing hour-long ascent. The marina is a good place to rent a boat, the best way of reaching the otherwise difficult-to-get-to bays and inlets along the coast.

Coop Marina della Lobra BOATING
(☑ 081 808 93 80; www.marinalobra.com; Marina della Lobra; per hour from €30) A reliable boat-

hire outfit, operating out of a kiosk by the car park. It also runs tours of Capri (€45).

🛏 Sleeping

★**Casale Villarena** APARTMENT €
(☑ 081 808 17 79; www.casalevillarena.it; Via Cantone 3, Nerano; 2-/4-person apt from €70/170; ⊙ Easter-Oct; P ⚹) These family-friendly apartments have good facilities, including a shared pool, a playground and a lovely beach within easy strolling distance. There are landscaped terraces with lemon trees, shady pergolas and such practical necessities as a laundry. The original property dates from the 18th century, but the apartments are comfortable, spacious and simply, yet elegantly, furnished.

★**Hotel Ristorante Primavera** HOTEL €
(☑ 081 878 91 25; www.laprimavera.biz; Via IV Novembre 3g; d €100; ⊙ Easter-Oct; ✳ 🛜) A welcoming, family-run two-star hotel, the Primavera has spacious, airy rooms with traditional Vietri tiles, light wood and white paint. Several rooms have terraces with sunbeds, plus table and chairs (rooms 101 to 103 are good choices). The bath tubs, in most rooms, are an unexpected treat. The bright terrace restaurant, with views stretching over orchards to the sea, serves typical local fare.

🍴 Eating

★**La Torre** SEAFOOD €€
(☑ 081 80 89 56; www.latorreonefire.it; Piazzetta Annunziata 7, Annunziata; meals €42; ⊙ 9am-midnight Mon & Wed-Thu, 9am-1am Fri-Sun Apr-Feb) 🍃 This delightful, laid-back Slow Food restaurant on a tranquil square serves mouthwatering traditional cuisine with an emphasis on seafood. The menu changes seasonally, but you can usually depend on classics like *tonani con patate* (tuna with potatoes). Consider the cholesterol-overdose indulgence of a nine-cheese taster (€6), ranging from fresh *caciottina* from Massa Lubrense to *provolone del Monaco* (seasoned semi-hard cheese).

Eat alfresco on the terrace, then stroll down to the belvedere for a rare wide-angle shot of Capri, Ischia, Procida, Naples and Vesuvius.

Funiculi Funiculá SEAFOOD €€
(Via Fontanelle 16, Marina della Lobra; meals €32; ⊙ noon-3pm Tue-Sun, plus 7-11.30pm Sat & Sun Apr-Oct; 🍴) This great bar-restaurant on the seafront at Marina della Lobra has views of Ischia, Capri and Vesuvius. Unsurprisingly,

the menu is dominated by seafood, but there are also family-friendly meal-in-one salads and the usual array of grilled-meat dishes. Pop next door to the cafe for a chocolate-filled crêpe or ice cream.

ℹ Information

Tourist Office (☑ 081 533 90 21; www.massa-lubrense.it; Viale Filangieri 11; ⊗ 9.30am-1pm daily, plus 4.30-8pm Mon, Tue & Thu-Sat) Can provide bus timetables and maps.

ℹ Getting There & Around

CAR

Massa Lubrense is an easy 20-minute drive from Sorrento. Parking is a matter of trawling the streets; there are some meters in the centre (€2 per hour).

Sant'Agata sui due Golfi

Sant'Agata sui due Golfi is the most famous of Massa Lubrense's 17 *frazioni*. It's a tranquil place that manages to retain its rustic charm despite a fairly heavy hotel presence.

For hikers, this area offers around 22 marked and well-maintained trails, stretching a total length of some 110km (66 miles). The tourist office can also provide details. If you fancy a relatively easy stroll that doesn't require a compass or hiking boots, there's a picturesque 3km trail between Sorrento and Sant'Agata. From Piazza Tasso in Sorrento, venture south along Viale Caruso and Via Fuorimura to pick up the Circumpiso footpath, marked in green on the walking maps available from tourist offices. The walk should take approximately one hour.

◉ Sights

Chiesa di Sant'Agata   CHURCH
(Piazza Sant'Agata; ⊗ 8am-1pm & 5-7pm) Located in the centre of the village, the cool decorative interior of this 17th-century parish church is famed for its polychrome marble altar, an exquisite work of inlaid marble, mother-of-pearl, lapis lazuli and malachite.

Convento del Deserto   MONASTERY, VIEWPOINT
(☑ 081 878 01 99; Via Deserto; ⊗ gardens 8am-7pm, lookout 10am-noon & 5-7pm summer, 10am-noon & 3-5pm winter) This Carmelite convent is located 1.5km uphill from the village centre, so read on carefully before striding out. It was founded in the 17th century and is still home to a closed community of Benedictine nuns. While the convent is of only moderate interest (unless you are one of the nuns), the 360-degree views really make the hike worthwhile.

🛏 Sleeping

Agriturismo Le Tore   AGRITURISMO €
(☑ 081 808 06 37; www.letore.com; Via Pontone 43; s €60-70, d €90-130, dinner €25-35; ⊗ Easter-early Nov; 🅿 @ 🛜) A working organic farm amid 14 hectares of olive groves, producing olive oil, sun-dried tomatoes (and paste) and marmalade (among other products), La Tore is a wonderful place to stay. Decidedly off the beaten track, it offers seven barnlike rooms within a lovely rustic farmhouse hidden among fruit trees. Terracotta tiles and wooden furniture add to the rural appeal.

Children between two and six years of age are offered a 50% discount (30% discount for seven- to 10-year-olds) if they sleep in their parents' room. During winter there is the option of a self-contained apartment. Additional meals are available.

CELEB-STYLE SEAFOOD

The only one of the marina's restaurants directly accessible from the sea, **Lo Scoglio** (☑ 081 808 10 26; www.hotelloscoglio.com; Piazza delle Sirene 15, Massa Lubrense; meals €60; ⊗ 12.30-5pm & 7.30-11pm) attracts a steady ripple of visiting celebs. Johnny Depp, Stephen Spielberg and Sienna Miller are all recent diners, while Elton John, Rod Stewart and Michael Caine have posed for pics (on display) in the past.

The locale is certainly memorable – a glass pavilion on a wooden jetty built around a kitsch fountain spurting into a pond full of fish – and the food is top notch (and priced accordingly). Although you can eat *ravioli alla caprese* and steak here, you'd be sorry to miss the superb seafood. Sample such saltwater specialities as a €30 antipasto of raw seafood on ice, followed by the local classic: *spaghetti al riccio* (spaghetti with sea urchins). Despite the whiff of glamour surrounding the clientele, this is an unpretentious, family-run place, complete with grandma keeping a watchful eye on the till.

Agriturismo Fattoria
Terranova
AGRITURISMO €

(☎081 533 02 34; www.fattoriaterranova.it; Via Pontone 10; d €85; ⊙Mar-Dec; [P][≋]) Stone floors, dried flowers hanging from heavy wooden beams and large wine barrels artfully positioned – this great *agriturismo* is the epitome of rural chic. The accommodation is in small apartments spread over the extensively cultivated grounds. The apartments are fairly simple, but the setting is delightful and the swimming pool is a welcome luxury.

✖ Eating

Lo Stuzzichino
NEAPOLITAN €

(☎081 533 00 10; www.ristorantelostuzzichino.it; Via Deserto 1a; tasting menu €40, meals €18, pizzas from €5; ⊙Feb-Dec) ✐ This Slow Food Movement–affiliated restaurant has a gregarious host in owner Paolo de Gregorio. Try the specialities: fish rolls stuffed with smoked cheese or seafood stew with seasonal vegetables. The rare *gamberetti di Crapolla* (prawns) taste a whole lot better than they sound.

★ Ristorante Don
Alfonso 1890
MEDITERRANEAN €€€

(☎081 533 02 26; www.donalfonso.com; Corso Sant'Agata 11; meals €115-125; ⊙closed Mon & Tue, except Tue night Jun-Sep, closed Jan-early Mar, Nov & Dec; [P]) This two-Michelin-star restaurant is generally regarded as one of Italy's finest. Prepared with produce from the chef's own 6-hectare farm, the seasonally changing menu includes such hallmark dishes as lightly seared tuna in red-pepper sauce and pasta with clams and zucchini. The international wine list is one of the country's most extensive and best. Reservations are essential. The restaurant is part of the hotel of the same name and also organises cooking courses.

ℹ Information

Tourist Office (☎081 533 01 35; www.santagatasuiduegolfi.it; Corso Sant'Agata 25; ⊙9am-1pm & 5.30-9pm) For information on the village and surrounding countryside, stop by this small office on the main square.

ℹ Getting There & Around

CAR
Follow the SS145 west from Sorrento for about 7km until you see signs off to the right. There is generally street parking available, although August can be busy, especially in the evening.

Marina del Cantone

Round the coast from Massa Lubrense, a beautiful hiking trail leads down from **Nerano** to the stunning **Baia de Ieranto** and Marina del Cantone.

⚐ Activities

A popular diving destination, the protected waters here are part of an 11-sq-km reserve called the **Punta Campanella**; it supports a healthy marine ecosystem, with flora and fauna flourishing in underwater grottoes.

Nettuno Diving
DIVING

(☎081 808 10 51; www.sorrentodiving.com; Via Vespucci 39; [♿]) Dive the depths of this marine reserve with a PADI-certified outfit that runs underwater activities for all ages and abilities. These include snorkelling excursions, beginner's courses, cave dives and immersions off Capri and the Li Galli islands. Costs start at €25 (children €15) for a day-long outing to the Baia de Ieranto. It can also organise reasonably priced accommodation.

🛏 Sleeping

Villaggio Residence
Nettuno
CAMPGROUND, APARTMENT €

(☎081 808 10 51; www.villaggionettuno.it; Via A Vespucci 39; camping per 2 people, tent & car €41, bungalows €130-185, apt €190; ⊙Mar-early Nov; [P][❄][@][🛜][≋]) Marina's campground – in the terraced olive groves by the entrance to the village – offers an array of accommodation options, including campsites, mobile homes and (best of all) apartments in a 16th-century tower for two to five people. It's a friendly, environmentally sound place with excellent facilities and a comprehensive list of activities.

EAST OF SORRENTO

More developed and less appealing than the coast west of Sorrento, the area to the east of town is not totally without interest. There's the district's longest sandy beach, Spiaggia di Alimuri, at Meta di Sorrento and the Roman villas at Castellammare di Stabia.

Rising above Castellammare and accessible by an eight-minute **cable-car ride** (adult/reduced €7/3.50; ⊙about 30 daily Apr-Oct) from the town's Circumvesuviana train station is Monte Faito (1131m), one of the highest peaks in the Lattari mountains. Covered in thick beech forests, the summit offers some fine walks with sensational views.

HISTORIC HAMLETS

Dotted around Vico's surrounding hills are a number of ancient hamlets, known as *casali*. Untouched by mass tourism, they offer a glimpse into a rural way of life that has changed little over the centuries. You will, however, need wheels to get to them. From Vico, take Via Roma and follow Via Rafaelle Bosco, which passes through the *casali* before circling back to town. Highlights include **Massaquano** and the Capella di Santa Lucia (open on request), famous for its 14th-century frescoes from the school of Giotto di Bondone (recognised as the forerunner of modern Western painting). **Moiano** is also worth checking out; an ancient path from here leads to the summit of Monte Faito. And then there is **Santa Maria del Castello**, with its fabulous views towards the southeast.

Three kilometres to the west of Vico, **Marina di Equa** stands on the site of the Roman settlement of Aequa. Among the bars and restaurants lining the popular pebble beaches are the remains of the 1st-century-AD Villa Pezzolo, as well as a defensive tower, the Torre di Caporivo, and the Gothic ruins of a medieval limestone quarry.

Vico Equense

Known to the Romans as Aequa, Vico Equense (Vico) is a small cliff-top town about 10km east of Sorrento.

◉ Sights

Chiesa dell'Annunziata CHURCH
(Via Vescovado; ☺ 10am-noon Sun) Vico's cliff-top former cathedral is the only Gothic church on the Sorrento Peninsula. Little remains of the original 14th-century structure other than the lateral windows near the main altar and a few arches in the aisles. In fact, most of what you see today, including the chipped pink-and-white facade, is 17th-century baroque.

In the sacristy, check out the portraits of Vico's bishops, all of whom are represented here except for the last one, Michele Natale, who was executed for supporting the ill-fated 1799 Parthenopean Republic. His place is taken by an angel with its finger to its lips, an admonishment to the bishop to keep his liberal thoughts to himself.

✖ Eating

Ristorante & Pizzeria da Gigino PIZZA
(☎ 081 879 83 09; www.pizzametro.it; Via Nicotera 15; pizza per metre €12-26; ☺ noon-1am; 🖩) Run by the five sons of pizza king Gigino Dell'Amura, who was the very first to introduce pizza by the metre to the world, this barnlike pizzeria produces kilometres of pizza each day in three huge ovens to the right of the entrance. There's a large selection of toppings and the quality is a crust above the norm. Although it seats around 200, you may still have to wait for a table. No reservations are taken.

❶ Information

Tourist Office (☎ 081 801 57 52; www.vico turismo.it; Piazza Umberto I; ☺ 9am-2pm & 3-8pm Mon-Sat, 9.30am-1.30pm Sun) General information on the area's attractions is available from this helpful office on the main square.

CAPRI

POP 14,100

The most visited of the islands in the Bay of Naples, Capri deserves more than a quick day trip. Beyond the glamorous veneer of chichi cafes and designer boutiques is an island of rugged seascapes, desolate Roman ruins and a surprisingly unspoiled rural inland.

Ferries dock at Marina Grande, from where it's a short funicular ride up to Capri, the main town. A further bus ride takes you up to Anacapri.

◉ Sights

Grotta Azzurra CAVE
(Blue Grotto; admission €13; ☺ 9am-1hr before sunset) Capri's single most famous attraction is the Grotto Azzura, a stunning sea cave illuminated by an other-worldly blue light.

The easiest way to visit is to take a tour from Marina Grande. This costs €26.50, comprising the return boat trip, a rowing boat into the cave and the cave's admission fee. Allow a good hour.

Giardini di Augusto GARDENS
(Gardens of Augustus; admission €1; ☺ 9am-1hr before sunset) Escape the crowds by seeking out these colourful gardens near the 14th-century Certosa di San Giacomo. Founded by the Emperor Augustus, they rise in a

SOOTHING ISLAND HIKES

Away from the boutiques, yachts and bikinis, Capri offers some soul-lifting hikes. Favourite routes include from Arco Naturale to the Punta dell'Arcera (1.2km, 1¼ hours), best tackled in this direction to avoid a final climb up to Arco Naturale. Another popular route is from Anacapri to Monte Solaro (2km, two hours), the island's highest point. If you don't fancy an upward trek, take the *seggiovia* (chairlift) up and walk down.

series of flowered terraces to a viewpoint offering breathtaking views over to the **Isole Faraglioni**, a group of three limestone stacks that rise vertically out of the sea.

Villa Jovis   RUIN

(Jupiter's Villa; Via Amaiuri; admission €2; ☺9am-1pm, closed Tue 1st-15th of month, closed Sun rest of month) Some 2km east of Capri along Via Tiberio, Villa Jovis was the largest and most sumptuous of the island's 12 Roman villas and Tiberius' main Capri residence. A vast pleasure complex, now reduced to ruins, it famously pandered to the emperor's debauched tastes, and included imperial quarters and extensive bathing areas set in dense gardens and woodland.

★ Seggiovia del Monte Solaro   CHAIRLIFT

(☑081 837 14 38; www.capriseggiovia.it; single/return €7.50/10; ☺9.30am-5pm summer, to 3.30pm winter) A fast and painless way to reach Capri's highest peak, Anacapri's Seggiovia del Monte Solaro chairlift whisks you to the top of the mountain in a tranquil, beautiful ride of just 12 minutes. The views from the top are outstanding – on a clear day, you can see the entire Bay of Naples, the Amalfi Coast and the islands of Ischia and Procida.

🛏 Sleeping & Eating

Hotel Villa Eva   HOTEL €€

(☑081 837 15 49; www.villaeva.com; Via La Fabbrica 8; d €100-160, tr €150-210, apt per person €55-70; ☺Easter-Oct; ✳🛜🏊) Nestled amid fruit and olive trees in the countryside near Anacapri, Villa Eva is an idyllic retreat, complete with swimming pool, lush gardens and sunny rooms and apartments. Stained-glass windows and vintage fireplaces add character, while the location ensures peace and quiet.

Hotel La Tosca   PENSION €€

(☑081 837 09 89; www.latoscahotel.com; Via Dalmazio Birago 5; s €50-100, d €75-160; ☺Apr-Oct; ✳🛜) Away from the glitz of Capri's town centre, this charming one-star place is hidden down a quiet back lane overlooking the Certosa di San Giacomo. The rooms are airy and comfortable, with pine furniture, light tiles, striped fabrics and large bathrooms. Several also have private terraces.

Lo Sfizio   TRATTORIA, PIZZA €€

(☑081 837 41 28; Via Tiberio 7; pizzas €7-11, meals €30; ☺noon-3pm & 7pm-midnight Wed-Mon Apr-Dec) On the path up to Villa Jovis, this trattoria-cum-pizzeria is ideally placed for a post-sightseeing meal. It's a relaxed, down-to-earth place with a few roadside tables and a typical island menu, ranging from pizza and handmade pasta to grilled meats and baked fish.

Pulalli   RISTORANTE €€

(☑081 837 41 08; Piazza Umberto 1; meals €35-40; ☺noon-3pm & 7-11.30pm daily Aug, closed Tue Sep-Jul) Climb Capri's clock-tower steps to the right of the tourist office and your reward is this lofty local hang-out where fabulous wine meets a discerning selection of cheese, charcuterie, and more substantial fare such as *risotto al limone* (lemon risotto). Try for a seat on the terrace or, best of all, the coveted table on its own balcony.

❶ Information

Information is available online at www.capritourism.com or from one of the three tourist offices: **Marina Grande** (☑081 837 06 34; www.capritourism.com; Quayside, Marina Grande; ☺9am-2pm & 3-6.50pm Mon-Sat, 9am-1pm & 2-7pm Sun), **Capri Town** (☑081 837 06 86; www.capritourism.com; Piazza Umberto I; ☺9am-7pm Mon-Sat, 9am-1pm & 2-7pm Sun) or **Anacapri** (☑081 837 15 24; www.capritourism.com; Via Giuseppe Orlandi 59, Anacapri; ☺9am-3pm).

❶ Getting There & Around

There are year-round boats to Capri from Naples and Sorrento. Timetables and fare details are available online at www.capritourism.com.

From Sorrento Jetfoils cost €17 to €18.50, slower ferries €14.50.

On the island, buses run from Capri Town to/from Marina Grande, Anacapri and Marina Piccola. Single tickets cost €1.80 on all routes, including the funicular.

The Amalfi Coast

Deemed by Unesco to be an outstanding example of a Mediterranean landscape, the Amalfi Coast is a beguiling combination of great beauty and gripping drama.

Positano

POP 3900

Positano is the coast's most picturesque and photogenic town, with vertiginous houses tumbling down to the sea in a cascade of sun-bleached peach, pink and terracotta colours. No less colourful are its steep streets and steps lined with wisteria-draped hotels, smart restaurants and fashionable boutiques.

There's still a southern-Italian holiday feel about the place, with sunbathers eating pizza on the beach, kids pestering parents for gelati and chic women from Milan checking out the boutiques. The fashionista history runs deep: *moda Positano* was born here in the '60s and the town was the first in Italy to import bikinis from France.

There certainly is something special about the place and this is reflected, predictably, in the prices, which tend to be higher here than elsewhere on the coast.

PLAN YOUR ROUTE

1. **Amalfi Coast** (p17) Passing through Positano then along the coast to Vietri sul Mare, this trip encapsulates fabulously picturesque towns with dizzying hairpin turns.

◉ Sights & Activities

Positano's most memorable sight is its pyramidal townscape, with pastel-coloured houses arranged down the slope to **Spiaggia Grande**, the main beach. Although it isn't anyone's dream beach, with greyish sand covered by legions of bright umbrellas, the water's clean and the setting is memorable. Hiring a chair and umbrella on the fenced-off areas costs around €18 per person per day, but the crowded public areas are free.

Getting around town is largely a matter of walking. If your knees can take the slopes, there are dozens of narrow alleys and stairways that make walking relatively easy and joyously traffic free. The easy option is to take the local bus to the top of the town for the best views, and wind your way down on foot, via steps and slopes, enjoying the memorable vistas en route.

Chiesa di Santa Maria Assunta CHURCH
(Piazza Flavio Gioia; ⊙8am-noon & 4-9pm) This church, with its colourful majolica-tiled dome, is the most famous and – let's face it – pretty much the only sight in Positano. If you are visiting at a weekend you will probably have the added perk of seeing a wedding; it's one of the most popular churches in the area for exchanging vows.

Step inside to see a delightful classical interior, with pillars topped with gilded Ionic capitals and winged cherubs peeking from above every arch. Above the main altar is a 13th-century Byzantine Black Madonna and Child.

Positano

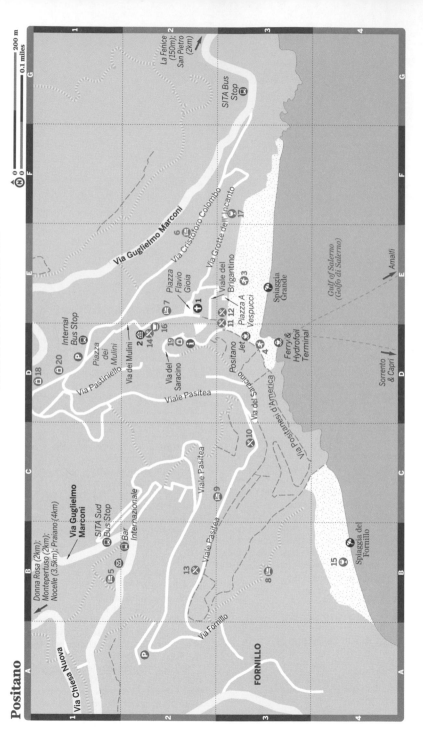

Donna Rosa (2km);
Montepertuso (2km);
Nocelle (3.5km); Praiano (4km)

Via Chiesa Nuova

Via Guglielmo Marconi

SITA Sud
Bus Stop

Bar
Internazionale

5

18
20

Internal
Bus Stop

Via Pastiniello

Piazza
dei
Mulini

Via dei Mulini

2 14

16
19

Via del Saracino

Viale Pasitea

Via Guglielmo Marconi

Piazza
Flavio
Gioia

6

7

1

Via Cristoforo Colombo

Via Grotte dell'Incanto

17

Viale del
Brigantino

3

11 12

Piazza A
Vespucci

Positano
Jet

Spiaggia
Grande

4

Ferry &
Hydrofoil
Terminal

Via del Saracino

Via Positanesi d'America

10

Viale Pasitea

9

13

8

Via Pasitea

Via Formillo

FORNILLO

15

Spiaggia del
Fornillo

La Fenice
(150m);
San Pietro
(2km)

SITA Bus
Stop

Gulf of Salerno
(Golfo di Salerno)

Amalfi

Sorrento
& Capri

N
200 m
0.1 miles

Positano

During restoration works of the square and the crypt, a Roman villa was discovered; still under excavation, it is closed to the public.

Franco Senesi GALLERY
(☑089 87 52 57; www.francosenesifineart.com; Via dei Mulini 16; ⊙10am-midnight Apr-Nov) Nestled between the colourful boutiques and lemon-themed ceramics shops, Franco Senesi is an airy exhibition space with several rooms showcasing over 20 Italian modern artists and sculptors. You can walk around here without being hassled, admiring artworks that are sufficiently varied to suit most tastes, spanning exquisite life drawings, colourful surrealistic landscapes and edgy abstract sculptures. Shipping can be arranged.

Palazzo Murat PALACE
(☑089 875 51 77; www.palazzomurat.it; Via dei Mulini 23) Just west of the Chiesa di Santa Maria Assunta church, this *palazzo* is now a luxury hotel. It may be beyond your budget to stay, but you can still visit the stunning flower-filled courtyard, have a drink in the vine-draped patio and contemplate the short, tragic life of flamboyant Joachim Murat, the 18th-century French king of Naples who had the palace built as a summer residence for himself and his wife, Caroline Bonaparte.

★**Blue Star** BOATING
(☑089 81 18 88; www.bluestarpositano.it; Spiaggia Grande; ⊙8.30am-9pm) Operating out of a kiosk on Spiaggia Grande, Blue Star hires out small motor boats for €60 per hour (€200 for four hours). Consider heading for the archipelago of Li Galli, the four small islands where, according to Homer, the sirens lived. The company also organises popular

and fun yacht excursions to Capri and the Grotta dello Smeraldo (€60).

L'Uomo e il Mare BOATING
(☑089 81 16 13; www.gennaroesalvatore.it; ⊙9am-8pm) An Italian-English couple offers a range of tours, including Capri and Amalfi day trips (from €55), out of a kiosk near the ferry terminal. They also run a romantic sunset cruise to Li Galli, complete with champagne (€30).

⊨ Sleeping

Villa Nettuno HOTEL €
(☑089 87 54 01; www.villanettunopositano.it; Viale Pasitea 208; s/d €70/85; ⊙year-round) Hidden behind a barrage of perfumed foliage, Villa Nettuno oozes charm. Go for one of the original rooms in the 300-year-old part of the building with heavy rustic decor and a communal terrace. Rooms in the renovated part of the villa lack the same character.

Pensione Maria Luisa PENSION €
(☑089 87 50 23; www.pensionemarialuisa.com; Via Fornillo 42; d €70-80, with sea view €95; ⊙Mar-Oct; @🖙) The Maria Luisa is a friendly old-school *pensione*. Rooms feature shiny blue tiles and simple, no-frills decor; those with private balconies are well worth the extra €15 for the bay views. If you can't bag a room with a view, there's a small communal terrace offering the same sensational vistas.

Hostel Brikette HOSTEL €
(☑089 87 58 57; www.hostel-positano.com; Via Marconi 358; dm €24-50, d €65-145, apt €80-220; ⊙year-round; ✳🖙) The Brikette is a bright, cheerful place with wonderful views and a range of sleeping options, from dorms to

doubles and apartments. Conveniently, it also offers a daily hostelling option that allows day trippers use of the hostel's facilities, including showers, wi-fi and left luggage, for €10. Breakfast isn't included. The English owner is a great source of information if you're planning walks in the area, providing maps and sound advice.

La Fenice B&B €€

(☑089 87 55 13; www.lafenicepositano.com; Via Guglielmo Marconi 4; d €140; ☉Easter-Oct; ☰) With hand-painted Vietri tiles, white walls and high ceilings, the rooms here are simple but stylish; most have their own balcony or terrace. The views are stunning, but it feels very smartly and not super posh. As with everywhere in Positano, you'll need to be good at stomping up and down steps to stay here. There's a delightful pool and hot tub, with even a little waterfall splashing from the rocks above.

Hotel California HOTEL €€

(☑089 87 53 82; www.hotelcaliforniapositano.it; Via Cristoforo Colombo 141; d €160-195; ☉Easter-Oct; ℗❉☎) Ignore the incongruous name: this Hotel California is housed in a grand 18th-century palace, its facade washed in soothing pinks and yellows. The rooms in the older part of the house are magnificent, with original ceiling friezes; new rooms are spacious and luxuriously decorated. Breakfast is served on a glorious and leafy front terrace.

★Hotel Palazzo Murat HOTEL €€€

(☑089 87 51 77; www.palazzomurat.it; Via dei Mulini 23; d €180-270; ☉May–mid-Jan; ❉@☎) Shielded behind an ancient wall from the tourists who surge along its pedestrian thoroughfare daily, this magnificent hotel occupies the

18th-century *palazzo* that the one-time king of Naples used as his summer residence. Rooms – five (more expensive) in the original part of the building, 25 in the newer section – are decorated with sumptuous antiques, original oil paintings and glossy marble. The lush gardens contain banana trees, bottlebrush, Japanese maple and pine trees.

★San Pietro HOTEL €€€

(☑089 87 54 55; www.ilsanpietro.it; Via Laurito 2; d from €420-580; ☉Apr-Oct; ℗❉☎☎) For such a talked-about hotel, the San Pietro is remarkably discreet. Built into a rocky headland 2km east of Positano, it's almost entirely below road level; if driving, look for an ivy-clad chapel and a black British telephone box by the side of the road. All the individually decorated rooms have sea views, private terrace and hot tub. Other facilities include a semicircular swimming pool, a Michelin-starred restaurant, and a private beach (accessible by lift) with an adjacent lawn and sunbeds, plus tennis court. The vast lobby is a suitably swish introduction and draped with brilliantly coloured bougainvillea – an unusual touch. There's a 24-hour complimentary shuttle service to Positano.

✖ Eating

La Brezza CAFE €

(☑089 87 58 11; www.labrezzapositano.it; Via Regina Giovanna 2; snacks around €6; ☉9am-1am; ☎) With a steely grey-and-white interior, free internet and wi-fi, and a terrace with views over the sea and quay, this is the best beachfront place for *panini* or snacks. There are regular art exhibitions and a daily 'happy hour' (6pm to 8pm), with drinks accompanied by complimentary light eats.

★Donna Rosa ITALIAN €€

(☑089 81 18 06; www.drpositano.com; Via Montepertuso 97-99, Montepertuso; meals from €40; ☉noon-2.30pm & 7-11.30pm Mon, Tue & Thu-Sun Apr-Dec, closed lunch Aug) This is one of the Amalfi Coast's most reputable restaurants, located in mountainside Montepertuso, above Positano. Once a humble trattoria and now run by Rosa's daughter Raffaella, the lineage is set to continue with Raffaella's daughter Erika, who studied with Jamie Oliver in London. The celebrity chef dined here on his honeymoon and declared it one of his favourite restaurants.

The menu changes frequently, but you can be guaranteed some of the best food – and views – on the coast. Don't miss the hot chocolate soufflé and be sure to book ahead. It also runs excellent cooking courses.

★Next2

RISTORANTE €€

(☎089 812 35 16; www.next2.it; Viale Pasitea 242; meals €45; ⊗6.30-11.30pm) Understated elegance meets creative cuisine at this contemporary set-up. Local and organic ingredients are put to impressive use in beautifully presented dishes such as ravioli stuffed with aubergine and prawns or sea bass with tomatoes and lemon-scented peas. Desserts are wickedly delicious, and the alfresco sea-facing terrace is summer perfection.

La Cambusa

SEAFOOD €€

(☎089 81 20 51; www.lacambusapositano.com; Piazza A Vespucci 4; meals €40; ⊗noon-midnight Mar-Nov) This restaurant, run by amiable Luigi, is on the front line, which, given the number of cash-rich tourists in these parts, could equal high prices for less-than-average food. Happily, that is not the case here. The locals still rate La Cambusa as a top place for seafood.

Go for simple spaghetti with clams, oven-baked sea bass or splash out with the Mediterranean lobster. There is a good selection of side dishes, like roasted artichokes, and the position is Positano at its best.

Da Vincenzo

ITALIAN €€

(☎089 87 51 28; www.davincenzo.it; Viale Pasitea 172-178; meals €40; ⊗noon-2.30pm & 6-11pm Wed-Mon, 6.30-11pm Tue) Superbly prepared dishes are served here by the third generation of restaurateurs. The emphasis is on fish dishes, which range from the adventurous, like grilled octopus tentacles skewered with deep-fried artichokes, to seasonal pasta dishes such as spaghetti with broad beans and fresh ricotta. Be sure to try co-owner Marcella's legendary desserts, considered the best in town. Reservations recommended.

You can also enjoy twanging Neapolitan guitarists during the summer months.

Ristorante Max

ITALIAN €€

(☎089 87 50 56; www.ristorantemax.it; Via dei Mulini 22; meals €40; ⊗9am-11pm Mar-Nov) Here you can peruse the gorgeously cluttered artwork (in lieu of a sea view) while choosing your dish. This upmarket restaurant and wine bar serves such dishes as sautéed clams and mussels, and zucchini flowers stuffed with ricotta and salmon. Cooking courses are available in summer.

☿ Drinking & Nightlife

Unless the idea of parading up and down town with a cashmere sweater draped over your shoulders turns you on, Positano's nightlife, overall, is not going to do much for you. More piano bar than warehouse, with a handful of exceptions, it's genteel, sophisticated and safe.

La Zagara

CAFE

(☎089 812 28 92; www.lazagara.com; Via dei Mulini 8; cakes €3, panini €5; ⊗8am-midnight) Dating back to 1950, this is the quintessential Italian terrace, draped with foliage and flowers,

OLIVIERO OLIVIERI/ROBERTHARDING/GETTY IMAGES ©

A WALK TO FORNILLO

This gentle walk, with (hooray!) an acceptable number of steps, leads from Positano's main Spiaggia Grande to Spiaggia di Fornillo. Toss off the stilettos and don the trainers: Fornillo is more laid-back than its swanky *spiaggia* (beach) neighbour and is also home to a handful of summer beach bars, which can get quite spirited after sunset.

To reach here, head for the western end of Spiaggia Grande, by the ferry harbour, and climb the steps. Walk past the Torre Trasita, one of the coast's many medieval watchtowers built to warn inhabitants of pirate raids and now a private residence. Continue on as the path passes dramatic rock formations, tiny inlets of turquoise water and bobbing boats until you reach the appealing Fornillo beach in time to enjoy a long, cold drink or multiscoop ice cream.

with an offshoot bar and superb *pasticceria* (pastry shop), elderly red-vested waiters, Neapolitan background music and some great Positano poseur-watching potential. Enjoy sumptuous creamy cakes as well as savoury snacks. There's live music in summer.

Music on the Rocks   CLUB
(☑ 089 87 58 74; www.musicontherocks.it; Via Grotte dell'Incanto 51; cover €10-30; ☺ 10pm-late) This is one of the town's few genuine nightspots and one of the best clubs on the coast. Music on the Rocks is dramatically carved into the tower at the eastern end of Spiaggia Grande. Join the flirty, good-looking crowd and some of the region's top DJs spinning mainstream house and reliable disco.

Da Ferdinando   BAR
(☑ 089 87 53 65; Spiaggia dei Fornillo; ☺ 10am-3am May-Oct) This summer-only beach bar rents out sun loungers and serves drinks and light snacks. The music is designed to make sure you shift into suitable party mood after sunset.

🛍 Shopping

La Bottego di Brunella   FASHION
(☑ 089 87 52 28; www.brunella.it; Viale Pasitea 72; ☺ 9am-9pm) This shop is one of the reasons local women always look so effortlessly chic. It is one of just a handful of boutiques where the clothes are designed and made in Positano (most boutiques import despite the sometimes-deceptive labelling). The garments here are made from pure linen and silks, the colours earthy shades of cream, ochre, brown and yellow.

There are two other branches in town, including a smaller boutique opposite Palazzo Murat.

La Botteguccia de Giovanni   SHOES
(☑ 089 81 18 24; www.labottegucciapositano.it; Via Regina Giovanni 19; ☺ 9.30am-9pm May-Oct) Come here for handmade leather sandals by craftsman Giovanni in his small workroom at the back of the shop. Choose the colour and any decorative bits and pieces you want (shells are particularly well suited to Positano somehow…), tell him your size and then nip round the corner for a cappuccino while he makes the shoes. Prices start at around €50.

Umberto Carro   CERAMICS
(☑ 089 87 53 52; Viale Pasitea 30; ☺ 9.30am-8.30pm May-Oct) On offer here is a sumptuous display of locally produced ceramics to stress you – and your hand luggage – at check-in time; a better bet is to go for the shipping option. The colours and designs are subtle and classy, and there's a wide range of pieces, from magnificent urns to minute eggcups and quirky, brightly coloured animals and ornaments.

ℹ Information

Tourist Office (☑ 089 87 50 67; Via del Saracino 4; ☺ 9am-7pm Mon-Sat, to 2pm Sun summer, 9am-4pm Mon-Sat winter) Can provide lots of information; expect to pay for walking maps and similar.

ℹ Getting There & Away

CAR & MOTORCYCLE

Take the A3 autostrada to Vietri sul Mare and then follow the SS163 coastal road. To hire a scooter, try **Positano Rent a Scooter** (☑ 089 812 20 77; www.positanorentascooter.it; Viale Pasitea 99; per day from €60). Don't forget that you will need to produce a driving licence and passport.

Parking

Parking here is no fun in summer. There are some blue-zone parking areas (€3 per hour) and a handful of expensive private car parks. **Parcheggio da Anna** (Viale Pasitea 173; per day €18) is located just before the Pensione Maria Luisa, at the top of town. Nearer the beach and town centre, **Di Gennaro** (Via Pasitea 1; per day €23) is near the bottom of Via Cristoforo Colombo.

Praiano

POP 1900

Praiano is 120m above sea level, and exploring involves lots of steps. There are also several trails that start from town, including a scenic walk – particularly stunning at sunset – that leaves from beside the San Gennaro church, descending due west to the **Spiaggia della Gavitelli** beach (via 300 steps), and carrying on to the medieval defensive Torre di Grado. The town is also a starting point for the Sentiero degli Dei.

◉ Sights & Activities

Marina di Praia   HARBOUR

Located a couple of kilometres east of the centre, this charming small beach and harbour are why most people stop off here. From the SS163 (next to the Hotel Onda Verde), a steep path leads down the cliffs to a tiny inlet with a small stretch of coarse sand and very tempting water; the best water is actually off the rocks, just before you get to the bottom. You can also rent boats here. In what were once fishermen's houses, there are now four restaurants, including an excellent place for seafood.

Centro Sub Costiera Amalfitana   DIVING

(☑089 81 21 48; www.centrosub.it; Via Marina di Praia; dives from €80; ⓓ) This well-respected local dive outfit offers lessons for adults and children over eight years, as well as night dives and full diving days with snacks on board.

🛏 Sleeping

Hotel Onda Verde   HOTEL €€

(☑089 87 41 43; www.hotelondaverde.com; Via Terramare 3, Praiano; d €110-230; ⓢApr-Nov; ✳🛜) This hotel enjoys a stunning cliffside position overlooking the picturesque Marina de Praiano. The interior is tunnelled into the stone cliff face, which makes it wonderfully cool in the height of summer. Rooms have lashings of white linen, satin bedheads, elegant Florentine-style furniture and majolica-tiled floors. Some have terraces with deckchairs for contemplating that view. The restaurant comes highly recommended.

Hotel Villa Bellavista   HOTEL €€

(☑089 87 40 54; www.villabellavista.it; Via Grado 47, Praiano; r €80-120; ⓢApr-Oct; ✳🛜⚟) Amid lush gardens that include a vast vegetable plot, this Praiano hotel has an old-fashioned charm with its slightly stuffy furniture in the public areas and large, cool but fairly bare rooms. The appeal lies in the fabulous views from the spacious, flower-festooned terrace; the delightful pool, surrounded by greenery; and the tranquil setting.

Located on a narrow lane that leads to the Spiaggia della Gavitelli, the (signposted) hotel is accessed via Via Rezzolo from the SS163 that runs through town.

✘ Eating

Da Armandino   SEAFOOD €€

(☑089 87 40 87; www.trattoriadaarmandino.it; Via Praia 1, Marina di Praia; meals €35; ⓢ1-4pm & 7pm-midnight Apr-Nov; ⓓ) Seafood lovers should head for this widely acclaimed, no-frills restaurant located in a former boatyard on the beach at Marina di Praia. Da Armandino is great for fish fresh off the boat. There's no menu; just opt for the dish of the day – it's all excellent.

The holiday atmosphere and appealing setting – at the foot of sheer cliffs towering up to the main road – round things off nicely.

Onda Verde   ITALIAN €€

(☑089 87 41 43; www.hotelondaverde.it; Via Terramare 3; meals €38; ⓢ1-2.30pm & 7.30-9.30pm Apr-Nov) Part of a hotel of the same name, this restaurant is located halfway down the steep steps leading to the marina (just beyond the defensive tower). Sit outside for the best views of the bay. The food here reflects an innovative take on traditional cuisine and includes a plentiful salad choice – just the thing on a sizzling summer's day.

La Brace   ITALIAN €€

(☑089 87 42 26; www.labracepraiano.com; Via G Capriglione; pizzas from €5, meals €25; ⓢ12.30-3pm & 6.30-10.30pm Mon, Tue & Thu-Sun) Located on the main street in town, this long-established restaurant has a decent reputation for seafood and pizzas. The dining room has sweeping views over the rooftops to the sea, and owner Gianni greets everyone like an old friend – in Italian, naturally; it's a favourite haunt of locals.

🍷 Drinking & Nightlife

★Africana   CLUB

(☑089 81 11 71; www.africanafamousclub.com; ⓢ7.30pm-3am May-Sep) This club near Marina di Praia makes for a memorable boogie – though beware the pricey drinks. Africana

Furore

has been going since the '50s, when Jackie Kennedy was just one of the famous VIP guests. It has an extraordinary cave setting, complete with natural blowholes and a glass dance floor so you can see fish swimming under your feet.

Shuttle buses run regularly from Positano, Amalfi and Maiori during summer. You can also catch a water taxi (€10) with **Positano Boats** (☑339 2539207; www.positano boats.info).

Furore

Originally founded by Romans fleeing barbarian incursions, Marina di Furore, a tiny fishing village, was once a busy little commercial centre, although it's difficult to believe that today. In medieval times its unique natural position freed it from the threat of foreign raids and provided a ready source of water for its flour and paper mills.

To get to upper Furore by car, follow the SS163 and then the SS366 signposts to Agerola.

Amalfi

POP 5428

Once a maritime superpower, today the permanent population of Amalfi is a fairly modest 5000 or so. The numbers swell significantly during summer, when day trippers pour in by the coachload.

Just around the headland, neighbouring **Atrani** is worth a trip for its lively piazza and popular beach; don't miss it.

◉ Sights & Activities

First stop is Piazza del Duomo, the town's focal-point square, with its majestic cathedral. To glean a sense of the town's medieval history, be sure to explore the narrow alleys parallel to the main street, with their steep stairways, covered porticoes and historic shrine niches.

Amalfi also has a beautiful seaside setting; it's the perfect spot for long, lingering lunches. If you're intent on going for a swim, you're better off hiring a boat and heading out to sea. You'll find a number of operators along Lungomare dei Cavalieri.

★**Cattedrale di Sant'Andrea**   CATHEDRAL
(☑089 87 10 59; Piazza del Duomo; ◔7.30am-7.45pm) A melange of architectural styles, Amalfi's cathedral, one of the few relics of the town's past as an 11th-century maritime superpower, makes a striking impression at the top of its sweeping flight of stairs. Between 10am and 5pm entrance is through the adjacent Chiostro del Paradiso, a 13th-century cloister.

The cathedral dates in part from the early 10th century and its stripy facade has been rebuilt twice, most recently at the end of the 19th century. The huge bronze doors merit a look – the first of their type in Italy, they were commissioned by a local noble and made in Syria before being shipped to Amalfi. Less impressive is the baroque interior, although the altar features some fine statues and there are some interesting 12th- and 13th-century mosaics.

Chiostro del Paradiso CHURCH

(☑089 87 13 24; Piazza del Duomo; adult/reduced €3/1; ⊗9am-7pm) To the left of Amalfi's cathedral porch, these magnificent Moorish-style cloisters were built in 1266 to house the tombs of Amalfi's prominent citizens; 120 marble columns support a series of tall, slender Arabic arches around a central garden. From the cloisters, go through to the **Basilica del Crocefisso**, where you'll find various religious artefacts displayed in glass cabinets and some fading 14th-century frescoes. Beneath lies the 1206 crypt containing the remains of Sant'Andrea.

Grotta dello Smeraldo CAVE

(admission €5; ⊗9.30am-4pm) Four kilometres west of Amalfi, this grotto is named after the eerie emerald colour that emanates from the water. Stalactites hang down from the 24m-high ceiling, while stalagmites grow up to 10m tall. Buses regularly pass the car park above the cave entrance (from where you take a lift or stairs down to the rowing boats). Alternatively, **Coop Sant'Andrea** (☑089 87 29 50; www.coopsantandrea.com; Lungomare dei Cavalieri 1) runs boats from Amalfi (€10 return, plus cave admission). Allow 1½ hours for the return trip.

Each year, on 24 December and 6 January, skin divers from all over Italy make their traditional pilgrimage to the ceramic *presepe* (nativity scene) submerged beneath the water.

★ Museo della Carta MUSEUM

(☑089 830 45 61; www.museodellacarta.it; Via delle Cartiere 23; admission €4; ⊗10am-6.30pm daily Mar-Oct, 10am-3.30pm Tue, Wed & Fri-Sun Nov-Feb) Amalfi's paper museum is housed in a rugged, cavelike 13th-century paper mill (the oldest in Europe). It lovingly preserves the original paper presses, which are still in full working order, as you'll see during the 15-minute guided tour (in English), which explains the original cotton-based paper production and the later wood-pulp manufacturing. Afterwards you may well be inspired to pick up some of the stationery sold in the gift shop, alongside calligraphy sets and paper pressed with flowers.

Amalfi Marine BOATING

(☑329 2149811; www.amalfiboats.it; Spiaggia del Porto, Lungomare dei Cavalieri) Run by American local resident Rebecca Brooks, Amalfi Marine hires out boats (without a skipper from €250 per day, per boat; maximum six passengers). It also organises day-long excursions along the coast and to the islands (from €45 per person).

🛏 Sleeping

Albergo Sant'Andrea HOTEL €

(☑089 87 11 45; www.albergosantandrea.it; Via Duca Mansone I; s/d €60/90; ⊗Mar-Oct; ❋🞲) Enjoy the atmosphere of busy Piazza del Duomo from the comfort of your own room. This modest two-star hotel has basic rooms with brightly coloured tiles and coordinating fabrics. Double glazing has helped cut down the piazza hubbub, which can reach fever pitch in high season – this is one place to ask for a room with a (cathedral) view.

Residenza del Duca HOTEL €€

(☑089 873 63 65; www.residencedelduca.it; Via Duca Mastalo II 3; s €70, d €130; ⊗Mar-Oct; ❋) This family-run hotel has just six rooms, all of them light, sunny, and prettily furnished with antiques, majolica tiles and the odd chintzy cherub. The Jacuzzi showers are excellent. Call ahead if you are carrying heavy bags, as it's a seriously puff-you-out-climb up some steps to reach here and a luggage service is included in the price. Room 2 is a particular winner, with its French windows and stunning views.

ART IN A TOWER

Torre a Mare (☑339 4401008; www. paolosandulli.com; Torre a Mare; ⊗9am-1pm & 3.30-7pm) Defensive towers sit all along the Amalfi Coast; ironically, they are generally known as Saracen towers, named after the very invaders they were erected to thwart. Although most lie empty, some are privately owned. At Marina di Praia you can combine a visit to one such tower, all while enjoying the original sculptures and artwork of Paolo Sandulli. Most distinctive are his 'heads' with the colourful sea-sponge hairdos. A spiral staircase leads to more works upstairs, including paintings. Paolo's work is on display throughout the Amalfi Coast, including at Positano's prestigious Palazzo Murat.

Amalfi

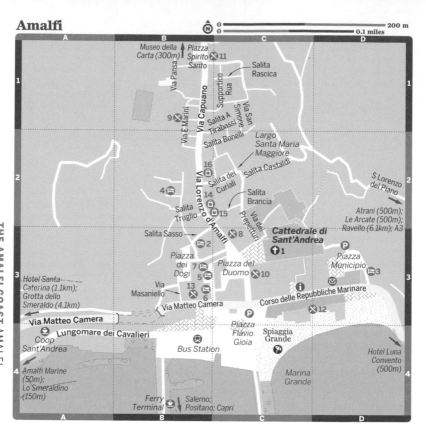

Amalfi

◉ Top Sights
1 Cattedrale di Sant'Andrea C3

◉ Sights
Chiostro del Paradiso .... (see 1)

🛏 Sleeping
2 Albergo Sant'Andrea B3
3 DieciSedici D3
4 Hotel Amalfi B2
5 Hotel Centrale B3
6 Hotel Lidomare B3
7 Residenza del Duca B3

✗ Eating
8 Da Maria C3
9 Il Teatro B1
10 La Pansa C3
11 La Taverna del Duca B1
12 Marina Grande D3
13 Ristorante La Caravella B3

🛍 Shopping
14 Anastasio Nicola Sas B2
15 Il Ninfeo C2
16 L'Arco Antico B2

Hotel Lidomare   HOTEL €€
(✆ 089 87 13 32; www.lidomare.it; Largo Duchi Piccolomini 9; s/d €65/145; ⊙ year-round; ❄ 🖧) Family
run, this old-fashioned hotel has real character. The large, luminous rooms have an air of
gentility, with their appealingly haphazard decor, vintage tiles and fine antiques. Some have
Jacuzzi bathtubs, others have sea views and
a balcony, some have both. Rather unusually,
breakfast is laid out on top of a grand piano.

Hotel Amalfi   HOTEL €€
(✆ 089 87 24 40; www.hamalfi.it; Vico dei Pastai 3;
s €70-120, d €100-120; ⊙ Easter-Oct; P ❄ 🖧) Located in the backstreets just off Amalfi's main

pedestrian thoroughfare, this family-run three-star hotel is elegant and central. Rooms, some of which have their own balconies, sport pale-yellow walls, majolica-tiled flooring and stencilling. The glossily tiled, albeit small, bathrooms have a choice of bath tub or shower. The roof garden is a relaxing place to idle over a drink.

Hotel Centrale
HOTEL €€

(☑089 87 26 08; www.amalfihotelcentrale.it; Largo Duchi Piccolomini 1; d €100-120; ⊙ Easter-Oct; ✴@🛜) This is one of the best-value hotels in Amalfi. The entrance is on a tiny little piazza in the *centro storico,* but many of the small but tastefully decorated rooms overlook Piazza del Duomo. The aquamarine ceramic tiling lends it a vibrant, fresh look and the views from the rooftop terrace are magnificent.

DieciSedici
B&B €€

(www.diecisedici.it; Piazza Municipio 10-16; d €150; ⊙ Easter-Oct; ✴) Brand new and brilliantly positioned, DieciSedici is located in a swishly renovated medieval palace. The bright rooms have tiled floors, whitewashed walls and – mostly – sea views. The friendly owners go out of their way to point you to good restaurants and attractions in the town. Satellite TV, air con and sound systems make it great value for money.

★Hotel Luna Convento
HOTEL €€€

(☑089 87 10 02; www.lunahotel.it; Via Pantaleone Comite 33; s €250-300, d €270-320, ste €460-620; ⊙ Easter-Oct; P✴@🛜⛱) This former convent was founded by St Francis in 1222 and has been a hotel for some 170 years. Rooms in the original building are in the former monks' cells, but there's nothing poky about the bright tiles, balconies and seamless sea views. The newer wing is equally beguiling, with religious frescoes over the bed. The cloistered courtyard is magnificent.

★Hotel Santa Caterina
HOTEL €€€

(☑089 87 10 12; www.hotelsantacaterina.it; Strada Amalfitana 9; d €315-770, ste from €480; ⊙ Mar-Oct; P✴🛜⛱) Situated west of town on the coastal road – and boasting fabulous views – this Amalfi landmark is one of Italy's most famous hotels. Everything here oozes luxury, from the discreet service to the fabulous gardens, the private beach to the opulent rooms. Built in 1880 by the Gambardella family, the hotel is run by the third generation of the same family.

For honeymooners, the Romeo and Juliet suite (€1000 to €3200 per night) is the one to go for, a private chalet in the colourful grounds.

✗ Eating & Drinking

La Pansa
CAFE €

(☑089 87 10 65; www.pasticceriapansa.it; Piazza del Duomo 40; cornetti & pastries from €1.50; ⊙ 8am-10pm Wed-Mon) A marbled and mirrored 1830 cafe on Piazza del Duomo where black-bow-tied waiters serve a great Italian breakfast: freshly made *cornetti* (croissants) and deliciously frothy cappuccino.

Il Teatro
TRATTORIA €€

(☑089 87 24 73; Via E Marini 19; meals €25; ⊙ 11.30am-3pm & 6.30-11pm, closed Wed; 🎰) Superb no-fuss trattoria tucked away in the atmospheric backstreets of the *centro storico* (Via E Marini is reached via Salita delgi Orafi). Seafood specialities include *pesce spada il teatro* (swordfish in a tomato, caper and olive-oil sauce), plus there are good vegetarian options, including *sciala-tielli al teatro* (pasta with tomatoes and aubergines). The old-fashioned interior has a series of arches and walls decorated with black-and-white photos and assorted bric-a-brac.

La Taverna del Duca
SEAFOOD €€

(☑089 87 27 55; www.amalfilatavernadelduca.it; Piazza Spirito Santo 26; pizzas from €7, meals €35; ⊙ noon-3pm & 7-11.30pm Fri-Wed) Grab a chair on the square at this popular restaurant with its fishy reputation. Specials vary according to the catch of the day but might include *carpaccio di baccalà* (thin strips of raw salted cod) or linguine with scampi. Or go for a pasta dish like *pasta fagioli e cozze* (with mussels and beans). There's an excellent and generous antipasti spread and the interior is elegant, with candles on the tables and tasteful oil paintings on the walls.

Da Maria
ITALIAN €€

(☑089 87 18 80; www.amalfitrattoriadamaria.com; Via Lorenzo d'Amalfi 16; pizzas around €6, meals €25; ⊙ noon-3pm & 7-11pm Dec-Oct; 🎰) Just off Piazza del Duomo, at the beginning of the

---

BEST COASTAL FOOD FESTIVALS

Sagra della Salsiccia e Ceppone (p75) Sorrento

Gustaminori (p102) Minori

Sagra del Tonno (p103) Cetara

SENTIERO DEGLI DEI (WALK OF THE GODS)

By far the best-known walk on the Amalfi Coast is the three-hour, 12km Sentiero degli Dei, which follows the high ridge linking Praiano to Positano. The walk commences in the heart of **Praiano**, where a thigh-challenging 1000-step start takes you up to the path itself. An easier alternative is to opt for the bus to **Bomerano**, near Agerola in the mountains between Sorrento and Amalfi: take the SITA bus to the Agerola turn-off, then another bus to Agerola. Bomerano is located immediately south of Agerola. Do consider the stepped route, though, which winds through well-tended gardens and makes for a charming start.

The route proper is not advised for vertigo sufferers: it's a spectacular, meandering trail along the top of the mountains, with caves and terraces set dramatically in the cliffs and deep valleys framed by the brilliant blue of the sea. It can sometimes be cloudy in the dizzy heights, but that somehow adds to the drama, with the cypresses rising through the mist like dark, shimmering sword blades and shepherds herding their goats through fog-wreathed foliage. Buy a picnic at the deli in Praiano to eat at the top (take a penknife for cheese and so on, as they don't make up rolls). Bring a rucksack and plenty of water and wear proper walking shoes, as the going is rough and the descents are steep. You may want to pack swimming gear too, and end the walk with a refreshing plunge into the sea.

The **Praiano tourist office** (☑089 87 45 57; www.praiano.org; Via G Capriglione 116b; ☺9am-1pm & 4-8pm) can provide maps and guidance. Just downhill and on the same side is **Alimentari Rispoli** (☑089 87 40 18; 82 Via Nazionale), where you can buy *panini*, cheeses, meat, drinks and fruit for the hike. The steps out of town begin at Via Degli Ulivi, which leads off the main road almost opposite Hotel Smereldo. Brace yourself for the long climb to come, and be sure to follow the brown arrows placed at regular intervals along the flower-edged paths. After around 45 minutes you'll emerge at **Fontanella**, at Chiesa

---

main pedestrian thoroughfare, this cavernous place attracts a dedicated crowd ranging from off-the-yacht Neapolitans to coachloads of tourists. But don't be put off, as the wood-fired pizzas are excellent, the atmosphere is jolly, and the pastas and main courses are solidly reliable, if a tad overpriced.

Lo Smeraldino   SEAFOOD €€
(☑089 87 10 70; www.ristorantelosmeraldino.it; Piazzale dei Protontini 1, Lungomare dei Cavalieri; pizzas around €9, meals €30; ☺11.45am-3pm & 6.45-11.15pm daily Jul & Aug, closed Tue Sep-Jun) Situated west of the centre, on the waterfront overlooking the fishing boats, this inviting blue-and-white beachside restaurant was founded in 1949. As well as crisp-based pizzas, this is a good place for fancy risottos, like smoked salmon and caviar, or simple classics like grilled or poached local fish.

Despite the location, this is not a place where you come wrapped in a sarong and wearing flip-flops; the atmosphere is one of understated elegance. Book ahead.

Le Arcate   ITALIAN €€
(☑089 87 13 67; www.learcate.net; Largo Orlando Buonocore, Atrani; pizzas from €6, meals €25; ☺12.30-3pm & 7.30-11.30pm Tue-Sun Sep-Jun, daily Jul & Aug; ✸) On a sunny day, it's hard to beat

the dreamy location: at the far eastern point of the harbour overlooking the beach, with Atrani's ancient rooftops and church tower behind you. Huge white parasols shade the sprawl of tables, while the dining room is a stone-walled natural cave. Pizzas are served at night; daytime fare includes risotto with seafood and grilled swordfish. The food is good, but it's a step down from the setting.

★Marina Grande   SEAFOOD €€€
(☑089 87 11 29; www.ristorantemarinagrande. com; Viale Delle Regioni 4; tasting menu lunch/dinner €25/60, meals €45; ☺noon-3pm & 6.30-11pm Tue-Sun Mar-Oct) ✔ Run by the third generation of the same family, this beachfront restaurant serves fish so fresh it's almost flapping. It prides itself on its use of locally sourced organic produce, which, in Amalfi, means high-quality seafood.

Ristorante La Caravella   ITALIAN €€€
(☑089 87 10 29; www.ristorantelacaravella.it; Via Matteo Camera 12; tasting menus €50-120; ☺noon-2.30pm & 7.30-11pm Wed-Mon; ✸) The regional food here recently earned the restaurant a Michelin star, with dishes that offer *nouvelle* zap, like black ravioli with cuttlefish ink, scampi and ricotta, or that are unabashedly simple, like the catch of the day served grilled

di Santa Maria a Castro, a lovely whitewashed chapel with a 15th-century fresco of the Madonna. You can also explore the spare chambers of the Convento San Domenico.

Just beyond you'll see a natural rock arch over the path to the right; don't go through it but continue uphill, where after around 20 minutes of steep terrain and craggy rock steps you'll come to the path proper, where you should take the turning to the left signed 'Positano Nocelle'. It's a long, delightful, gentle descent from here to Nocelle: if there's cloud cover the combination of this and the glimpses of dizzying views is unforgettable. The route is marked by red and white stripes daubed on rocks and trees and is easy to follow.

You eventually emerge at tiny **Nocelle**, where cold drinks and coffee are served at a charming terraced kiosk with fresh flowers on the tables. Or head a little further through the village to Piazza Santa Croce, where a stall dispenses fantastic freshly squeezed orange and lemon juice.

Continue down through the village and a series of steps will take you through the olive groves and deposit you on the road just east of Positano. A nicer though longer option – especially if you're weary of steps at this point – is to continue on the path that leads west out of Nocelle towards **Montepertuso**. Don't miss the huge hole in the centre of the cliff at Montepertuso, where it looks as though some irate giant has punched through the slab of limestone. From here the route winds its way to the northern fringes of **Positano**. From here you can dip down through town to the beachfront bars and balmy sea.

Hiking maps can be downloaded at www.amalficoastweb.com. Another reliable regional hiking map is the Club Alpino Italiano (CAI; Italian Alpine Club) *Monti Lattari, Peninsola Sorrentina, Costiera Amalfitana: Carta dei Sentieri* (€9) at 1:30,000. If you prefer a guided hike, there are a number of reliable local guides, including American Frank Carpegna (www. positanofrankcarpegna.com), a longtime resident here, and Zia Lucy (www.zialucy.it).

on lemon leaves. Wine aficionados are likely to find something to try on the 15,000-label list. Reservations are essential. This is one of the few places in Amalfi where you pay for the food rather than the location, which in this case is far from spectacular, sandwiched between the rushing traffic of the road and the old arsenal. But that doesn't worry the discreet, knowledgeable crowd who eat here.

🛍 Shopping

Il Ninfeo   CERAMICS
(☑ 089 873 63 53; www.amalficoastceramics.com; Via Lorenzo d'Amalfi 28; ☉ 9am-9pm) Unabashedly tourist-geared, Il Ninfeo has a vast showroom displaying an excellent selection of ceramics, ranging from giant urns to fridge magnets. If they're not too busy, ask whether you can see the fascinating remains of a Roman villa under the showroom. It makes you realise just how much is hidden under this town.

Anastasio Nicola Sas   FOOD, BEAUTY
(☑ 089 87 10 07; Via Lorenzo d'Amalfi 32; ☉ 9am-8.30pm) Unless you're flying long haul, gourmet goodies can make excellent gifts. In this upscale supermarket, among the hanging hams, you'll find a full selection, ranging from local cheese and preserves to coffee,

chocolate, *limoncello* and every imaginable shape of pasta. There's also a collection of fruit-scented soaps and natural shampoos, perfumes and moisturisers.

L'Arco Antico   SOUVENIRS
(☑ 089 873 63 54; Via Capuano 4; ☉ 9.30am-8.30pm) Amalfi's connection with paper making dates back to the 12th century, when the first mills were set up to supply the republic's small army of bureaucrats. Although little is made here now, you can still buy it and the quality is still good. This attractive shop sells a range of products, including beautiful writing paper, leather-bound notebooks and huge photo albums.

ℹ Information

Tourist Office (☑ 089 87 11 07; www.amalfi touristoffice.it; Corso delle Repubbliche Marinare 33; ☉ 9am-1pm & 2-6pm Mon-Sat)

ℹ Getting There & Away

CAR & MOTORCYCLE
If driving from the north, exit the A3 autostrada at Vietri sul Mare and follow the SS163. From the south, leave the A3 at Salerno and head for Vietri sul Mare and the SS163.

Atrani
LEOKS/SHUTTERSTOCK

Parking

Parking is a problem in this town, although there are some parking places on Piazza Flavio Gioia near the ferry terminal (€3 per hour), as well as an underground car park accessed from Piazza Municipio with the same hourly rate.

Ravello

POP 2500

Most people visit on a day trip from Amalfi – a nerve-tingling 7km drive up the Valle del Dragone – although, to best enjoy its romantic, otherworldly atmosphere, you'll need to stay here overnight. On Tuesday morning there's a lively street market in Piazza Duomo, where you'll find wine, mozzarella and olive oil, as well as discounted designer clothes.

◉ Sights

Duomo   CATHEDRAL

(Piazza Duomo; museum €3; ⊘8.30am-noon & 5.30-8.30pm) Forming the eastern flank of Piazza Duomo, the cathedral was built in 1086 but has since undergone various makeovers. The facade is 16th century, but the central bronze door, one of only about two dozen in the country, dates from 1179; the interior is a late-20th-century interpretation of what the original must once have looked like.

Of particular interest is the striking pulpit, supported by six twisting columns set on

marble lions and decorated with flamboyant mosaics of peacocks and other birds. Note also how the floor is tilted towards the square – a deliberate measure to enhance the perspective effect. Entry is via the cathedral museum, displaying a modest collection of religious artefacts.

★Villa Rufolo   GARDENS

(☑089 85 76 21; www.villarufolo.it; Piazza Duomo; adult/reduced €5/3; ⊘9am-5pm) To the south of Ravello's cathedral, a 14th-century tower marks the entrance to this villa, famed for its beautiful cascading gardens. Note that the gardens are at their best from May till October; they don't merit the entrance fee outside those times.

The villa was built in the 13th century for the wealthy Rufolo dynasty and was home to several popes as well as king Robert of Anjou. Wagner was so inspired by the gardens when he visited in 1880 that he modelled the garden of Klingsor (the setting for the second act of the opera *Parsifal*) on them. Today the gardens are used to stage concerts during the town's classical-music festival.

Villa Cimbrone   GARDENS

(☑089 85 80 72; www.villacimbrone.com; Via Santa Chiara 26; adult/reduced €7/4; ⊘9am-7.30pm summer, to sunset winter) Some 600m south of Piazza Duomo, the Villa Cimbrone is worth a wander, if not for the 11th-century villa itself (now an upmarket hotel), then for the fabulous views from the delightful gardens. They're best admired from the Belvedere of Infinity, an awe-inspiring terrace lined with classical-style statues and busts.

The villa was something of a bohemian retreat in its early days and was frequented by Greta Garbo and her lover Leopold Stokowski as a secret hideaway. Other illustrious former guests included Virginia Woolf, Winston Churchill, DH Lawrence and Salvador Dalí.

Auditorium Oscar Niemeyer   THEATRE

(☑346 7378561; Via della Repubblica 12) Located just below the main approach to town, this modern building has attracted a love-it-or-hate-it controversy in town. Designed by renowned Brazilian architect Oscar Niemeyer, it is characterised by the sinuous profile of a wave and approached via a rectangular exterior courtyard, which is typically the site of temporary exhibitions of world-class sculpture. The auditorium is a venue for concerts and exhibitions.

Ravello

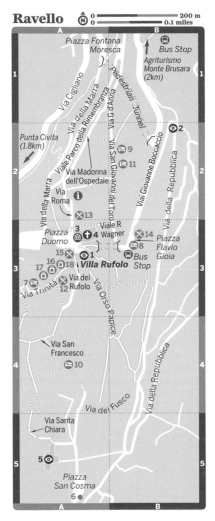

Ravello

Apparently Humphrey Bogart made a tradition out of having Mamma Agata's lemon cake (made with *limoncello*) for breakfast when she was cooking for a wealthy American family here back in the '60s. Other guests of this Hollywood-connected couple included Richard Burton, Frank Sinatra, Audrey Hepburn and, more recently, Pierce Brosnan. Price varies depending on the time of year.

✦ Festivals & Events

Ravello's program of classical music begins in March and continues until late October. It reaches its crescendo in June and September with the **International Piano Festival** and **Chamber Music Week**. Performances by top Italian and international musicians are world class, and the main venues are unforgettable. Tickets, bookable by phone or online, start at €25 (plus a €2 booking fee). For further information, contact the **Ravello Concert Society** (www.ravelloarts.org).

★ **Ravello Festival**   PERFORMING ARTS
(☎089 85 83 60; www.ravellofestival.com; ◷ Jun-Sep) Between late June and early September, the Ravello Festival – established in 1953 –

☚ Courses

★ **Mamma Agata**   COOKING COURSE
(☎089 85 70 19; www.mammaagata.com; Piazza San Cosma 9; courses Apr-Nov €200, May-Oct €250) Mamma Agata, together with her daughter Chiara, offers private cooking classes in her home, producing simple, exceptional food using primarily organic ingredients. A one-day demonstration class culminates in an interlude on a lovely sea-view terrace, tasting what you've been taught to make and enjoying homemade *limoncello*. There is also a cookbook available for purchase.

turns much of the town centre into a stage. Events range from orchestral concerts and chamber music to ballet performances; film screenings and exhibitions are held in atmospheric outdoor venues, most notably the famous overhanging terrace in the Villa Rufolo gardens.

🛏 Sleeping

Affitacamere Il Roseto   PENSION €

(☑ 089 858 64 92; www.ilroseto.it; Via Trinità 37; s €60-70, d €80-90; ⊙ year-round) If you're after a no-frills, clean room within easy walking distance of everything, come here. There are only two rooms, both of which have white walls, white sheets and white floors. But what they lack in charm they make up for in value, and, if you want colour, you can always sit outside under the lemon trees.

The owners also run the Profumi della Costiera *limoncello* shop.

Agriturismo Monte Brusara   AGRITURISMO €

(☑ 089 85 74 67; www.montebrusara.com; Via Monte Brusara 32; s/d €45/90; ⊙ year-round) An authentic working farm, this mountainside *agriturismo* is located a tough half-hour walk of about 1.5km from Ravello's centre (call ahead to arrange to be picked up). It is especially suited to families – children can feed the pony while you sit back and admire the views – or to those who simply want to escape the crowds.

The three rooms are comfy but basic, the food is fabulous and the owner is a charming, garrulous host. Half-board is also available.

★ Punta Civita   B&B €€

(☑ 089 872 326; www.puntacivita.it; Via Civita 4; d €110; ⊙ Mar-Oct; 🛜) Located on the road up to Ravello and accessible via a 15-minute walk from Atrani, this spruce little B&B has a bougainvillea-wreathed terrace with heavenly views of the sea and surrounding lemon groves, and bright tiled rooms that also look seaward. The warm, friendly owners serve an excellent Continental breakfast on – of course – the terrace.

Albergo Ristorante Garden   HOTEL €€

(☑ 089 85 72 26; www.gardenravello.com; Via Giovanne Boccaccio 4; s/d €140/160; ⊙ mid-Mar–late Oct; ❄🛜) Look at the photos behind reception to see the current owners playing with the Jackie Kennedy brood many years ago. Although no longer the celebrity magnet that it once was, this family-run three-star

is a good bet. The smallish rooms leave little impression (clean with nondescript decor), but the views are superb and fridges are a welcome touch. Apparently Gore Vidal was a regular at the terrace restaurant (meals from around €30).

Hotel Villa Amore   PENSION €€

(☑ 089 85 71 35; www.villaamore.it; Via dei Fusco 5; s/d €65/120; ⊙ May-Oct; @) This welcoming family-run *pensione* is the best choice in town by price. Tucked down a quiet lane, it has modest, homey rooms and sparkling bathrooms. All rooms have a balcony and some have bath tubs. The restaurant is a further plus, its terrace boasting fabulous views: the food's good and prices are reasonable (around €25 for a meal).

★ Hotel Caruso   HOTEL €€€

(☑ 089 85 88 01; www.hotelcaruso.com; Piazza San Giovanni del Toro 2; s €575-720, d €757-976; ⊙ Apr-Nov; P❄🛜♨) There can be no better place to swim than the Caruso's sensational infinity pool. Seemingly set on the edge of a precipice, its blue waters merge with sea and sky to magical effect. Inside, the sublimely restored 11th-century *palazzo* is no less impressive, with Moorish arches doubling as window frames, 15th-century vaulted ceilings and high-class ceramics. Rooms are suitably mod-conned: the TV/DVD system slides sexily out of a wooden cabinet at the foot of the bed.

Palazzo Avino   HOTEL €€€

(Palazzo Sasso; ☑ 089 81 81 81; www.palazzosasso. com; Via San Giovanni del Toro 28; d from €320, with sea view €530; ⊙ Mar-Oct; ❄🛜♨) One of three luxury hotels on Ravello's millionaires' row, Palazzo Sasso has been a hotel since 1880, sheltering many 20th-century luminaries – General Eisenhower planned the Allied attack on Monte Cassino here, and Roberto Rossellini and Ingrid Bergman flirted over dinner in the restaurant. A stunning pale-pink 12th-century palace, it combines tasteful antiques with Moorish colours and modern sculpture.

ℹ PARKING IN RAVELLO

The metered parking around the pedestrianised (ie car-free) centre of Ravello is obviously geared towards Ferrari owners: a costly €5 an hour and only payable by credit card. Alternatively, head for the underground car park at the Auditorium Oscar Niemeyer (p98).

Eating

Caffe Calce   CAFE **€**

(☑ 089 85 71 52; www.caffecalce.com; Viale Richard Wagner 3; ice creams €2; ☺ 8am-10pm) Located just above the Piazza Duomo, this place has a time-tested feel, with its old-fashioned interior and crusty local clientele. The coffee is famously the best in town, and the sweet treats of pastries and ice creams are good.

★ Babel   CAFE **€€**

(☑ 089 858 62 15; Via Trinità 13; meals €20; ☺ 11am-11pm) A cool little white-painted deli-cafe serving high-quality, affordable salads, bruschetta, cheese and meat boards and an excellent range of local wines. There's a jazz soundtrack, and a little gallery selling unusually stylish ceramic tiles.

Da Salvatore   ITALIAN **€€**

(☑ 089 85 72 27; www.salvatoreravello.com; Via della Republicca 2; meals €28; ☺ noon-3pm & 7.30-10pm Tue-Sun) Located just before the bus stop, Da Salvatore has nothing special by way of decor, but the view – from both the dining room and the large terrace – is very special indeed. Dishes include creative options like tender squid on a bed of pureed chickpeas with spicy *peperoncino* (chilli pepper). In the evening, part of the restaurant is transformed into an informal pizzeria, serving some of the best wood-fired pizza you will taste anywhere this side of Naples.

Ristorante Pizzeria Vittoria   PIZZA **€€**

(☑ 089 85 79 47; www.ristorantepizzeriavittoria.it; Via dei Rufolo 3; pizza from €5, meals €30; ☺ 12.15-3pm & 7.15-11pm; ⊕) Come here for exceptional pizza, with some 16 choices on the menu, including the Ravellese, with cherry tomatoes, mozzarella, basil and zucchini. Other dishes include lasagne with red pumpkin, smoked mozzarella and porcini mushrooms, and an innovative chickpea-and-cod antipasto. The atmosphere is one of subdued elegance, with a small outside terrace and grainy historical pics of Ravello on the walls

Shopping

Profumi della Costiera   DRINK

(☑ 089 85 81 67; www.profumidellacostiera.it; Via Trinità 37; ☺ 9am-8pm) The *limoncello* produced here is made with local lemons; known to experts as *sfusato amalfitano*, they're enormous – about double the size of

a standard lemon. The tot is made according to traditional recipes, so there are no preservatives and no colouring. All bottles carry the Indicazione Geografica Proteta (IGP; Protected Geographical Indication) quality mark. You may see the bottling in progress when you visit; it takes place at the back of the shop.

Wine & Drugs   FOOD

(☑ 089 85 84 43; Via Trinità 6; ☺ 9.30am-9.30pm) Despite the tongue-in-cheek name, no mind-altering substances are sold here, only grappa, organic olive oil, saffron and a good selection of local and international wines. There are also complimentary daily tastings of aged Parmesan dipped into similarly elderly 24-year-old balsamic vinegar.

Check out the owner's collection of baseball caps (over 400 at last count), sent by appreciative customers from around the world in exchange for a Ravello cap, which is routinely included in any shipment.

Cashmere   CLOTHING

(☑ 089 85 84 67; www.filodautoreravello.it; Via Trinità 8; scarves from €35; ☺ 9.30am-9pm) Although you may associate cashmere with more northern climes, this tiny shop in the Ravello backstreets is worth a visit to view the exceptional quality of the locally produced clothing, made primarily from pure cashmere, as well as linen.

ℹ️ Information

Tourist Office (☏ 089 85 70 96; www.ravello time.it; Via Roma 18; ⊙9am-7pm) Can assist with accommodation.

ℹ️ Getting There & Away

CAR

Turn north about 2km east of Amalfi. Vehicles are not permitted in Ravello's town centre, so consider parking nearby (p100).

Minori

POP 3000

About 3.5km east of Amalfi, or a steep 45-minute walk down from Ravello, Minori is a small, workaday town, popular with holidaying Italians. Much scruffier than its refined coastal cousins Amalfi and Positano, it's no less dependent on tourism yet seems more genuine, with its festive seafront, pleasant beach, atmospheric pedestrian shopping streets and noisy traffic jams. It is also known for its history of pasta making, dating back to medieval times, the speciality being *scialatielli* (thick ribbons of fresh pasta), featured on many local restaurant menus.

👁️ Sights

Villa Roma Antiquarium HISTORIC BUILDING
(☏089 85 28 93; Via Capodipiazza 28; ⊙8am-7pm) **FREE** Rediscovered in the 1930s, the 1st-century Villa Roma Antiquarium is a typical example of the splendid homes that Roman nobles built as holiday retreats in the period before Mt Vesuvius' AD 79 eruption. The best-preserved rooms surround the garden on the lower level, the highlight being a floor mosaic depicting a bull. There's also a two-room museum exhibiting various artefacts, including a collection of 6th-century-BC to 6th-century-AD amphorae.

⭐ Festivals & Events

Gustaminori FOOD
(⊙early Sep) Food lovers on the coast gather in Minori for the town's annual food jamboree, with pasta stalls (and the like) as well as live music.

🍴 Eating

Gambardella PASTRIES €
(☏089 87 72 99; www.gambardella.it; Piazza Cantilena 7; pastries from €1.50) This is the place to come for superb coffee and exemplary pastries – try the *sfogliatella* (ricotta-filled flaky pastry) and *torta di ricotta e pere* (ricotta and pear tart). You can buy *limoncello* and similar boozy delights made with wild strawberries, bilberries, bay leaves and wild fennel.

Il Giardiniello ITALIAN €€
(☏089 87 70 50; www.ristorantegiardiniello.com; Corso Vittorio Emanuele 17; pizza from €8, menu €30; ⊙noon-2.30pm & 7-11.30pm Thu-Tue) Easy

DANITA DELIMONT/GETTY IMAGES ©

Villa Rufolo, Ravello (p98)

THE AMALFI COAST MINORI

to find, just up from the seafront on a bustling pedestrian street, Giardiniello has been pleasing local palates since 1955. Sit on the terrace surrounded by fragrant jasmine and enjoy a 40cm pizza to share (€16) or a girth-expanding menu featuring town speciality *scialatielli* followed by local fish and dessert, plus wine.

ℹ Information

Tourist Office (☑ 089 87 70 87; www.proloco. minori.sa.it; Via Roma 30; ☺ 9am-noon & 5-8pm Mon-Sat, 9-11am Sun) Head for this small office on the seafront for general information and walking maps.

Cetara

POP 2400

Just beyond Erchie and its pleasant beach, Cetara is an important fishing centre. Recently, locals have resurrected the production of what is known as *colatura di alici*, a strong anchovy essence believed to be the descendant of *garum*, the Roman fish seasoning.

✤ Festivals & Events

Sagra del Tonno   FOOD
(☺ late Jul/early Aug) Each year the village celebrates *sagra del tonno*, a festival dedicated to tuna and anchovies. If you can time your visit accordingly, there are plenty of opportunities for tasting, as well as music and other general festivities. Further details are available from the tourist office. If you miss the festival, no worries: you can pick up a jar (never a tin) of the fishy specialities, preserved in olive oil, at local food shops and delis.

✕ Eating

Al Convento   SEAFOOD, PIZZA €€
(☑ 089 26 10 39; www.alconvento.net; Piazza San Francesco 16; meals €25; ☺ 12.30-3pm & 7-11pm summer, closed Wed winter) Al Convento enjoys an evocative setting in former church cloisters with original, albeit faded, 17th-century frescoes. This is an excellent spot to tuck into some local fish specialities: you can eat *tagliata di tonna alle erbe* (lightly grilled tuna with herbs) as an antipasto, and the spaghetti with anchovies and wild fennel is particularly delicious. For dessert, try the decadent chocolate cake with ricotta and cream.

ℹ Information

Tourist Office (☑ 328 0156347; Piazza San Francesco 15; ☺ 9am-1pm & 5pm-midnight) For accommodation and general info.

Vietri sul Mare

POP 8600

Vietri sul Mare is the ceramics capital of Campania. The unmistakable local style – bold brush strokes and strong Mediterranean colours – found favour in the royal court of Naples, which became one of Vietri's major clients. Later, in the 1920s and '30s, the arrival of international artists (mainly Germans) led to a shake-up of traditional designs. The *centro storico* is packed with decorative tiled-front shops selling ceramic wares of every description.

◉ Sights

Museo della Ceramica   MUSEUM
(☑ 089 21 18 35; Villa Guerriglia; ☺ 9am-3pm Tue-Sat, 9.30am-1pm Sun) FREE For a primer on Vietri's ceramics past, head to this museum in the nearby village of Raito. It has a comprehensive collection, including pieces from the 'German period' (1929–47), when the town attracted an influx of artists, mainly from Germany.

⬚ Shopping

Ceramica Artistica Solimene   CERAMICS
(☑ 089 21 02 43; www.ceramica solimene.it; Via Madonna degli Angeli 7; ☺ 9am-7pm Mon-Fri, 10am-1pm & 4-7pm Sat) This vast factory outlet, the most famous ceramics shop in town, sells everything from egg cups to ornamental mermaids, mugs to lamps. Even if you don't go in, it's worth having a look at the shop's extraordinary glass and cera mic facade. It was designed by Italian architect Paoli Soleri, who studied under the famous American 'organic' architect Frank Lloyd Wright.

Ceramiche Sara   CERAMICS
(☑ 089 21 00 53; www.ceramichesara.it; Via Costiera Amalfitana 14-16) Located at the entrance to town, and with a convenient car park, the showroom here has a great choice of ceramics, including some reasonably priced and colourful tiles (€8) that make terrific hotplates.

ℹ Information

Tourist Office (☑ 089 21 12 85; Piazza Matteotti; ☺ 10am-1pm & 5-8pm Mon-Fri, 10am-1pm Sat) This moderately helpful office is near the entrance to the *centro storico*.

Salerno & the Cilento

Don't miss the Cilento region, one of this area's lesser-known glories, with a largely undeveloped coastal strip and a beautiful national park famed for its orchids.

Salerno

POP 139,000

Upstaged by the glut of postcard-pretty towns along the Amalfi Coast, Campania's second-largest city is actually a pleasant surprise. A decade of civic determination has turned this major port and transport hub into one of southern Italy's most liveable cities, and its small but buzzing *centro storico* is a vibrant mix of medieval churches, tasty trattorias and good-spirited, bar-hopping locals.

◉ Sights

★ **Duomo** CATHEDRAL
(Piazza Alfano; ⊘ 9am-6pm Mon-Sat, 4-6pm Sun) You can't miss the looming presence of Salerno's impressive cathedral, widely considered to be the most beautiful medieval church in Italy. Built by the Normans in the 11th century and later aesthetically remodelled in the 18th

century, it sustained severe damage in a 1980 earthquake. It is dedicated to San Matteo (St Matthew), whose remains were reputedly brought to the city in 954 and now lie beneath the main altar in the vaulted crypt.

Take special note of the magnificent main entrance, the 12th-century **Porta dei Leoni**, named after the marble lions at the foot of the stairway. It leads through to a beautiful, harmonious courtyard, surrounded by graceful arches and overlooked by a 12th-century bell tower. Carry on through the huge bronze doors (similarly guarded by lions), which were cast in Constantinople in the 11th century. When you come to the three-aisled interior, you will see that it is largely baroque, with only a few traces of the original church. These include parts of the transept and choir floor and the two raised pulpits in front of the choir stalls. Throughout the church you can see extraordinarily detailed and colourful 13th-century mosaic work.

In the right-hand apse, don't miss the **Cappella delle Crociate** (Chapel of the Crusades), containing stunning frescoes and more wonderful mosaics. It was so named because crusaders' weapons were blessed here. Under the altar stands the tomb of 11th-century pope Gregory VII.

Castello di Arechi CASTLE
(☑ 089 296 40 15; www.ilcastellodiarechi.it; Via Benedetto Croce; adult/reduced €5/2.50; ⊘ 9am-7pm Tue-Sat, to 6.30pm Sun summer, to 5pm Tue-Sun winter) Hop on bus 19 from Piazza

---

PLAN YOUR ROUTE
....

3 **Southern Larder** (p37) Passing through Salerno on the way to Paestum, this trip explores Campania's raw beauty.

4 **Cilento Coastal Trail** (p45) From Paestum to Sapri, this rugged coastline boasts fascinating hilltop towns and ancient Greek ruins.

XXIV Maggio to visit Salerno's most famous landmark, the forbidding Castello di Arechi, dramatically positioned 263m above the city. Originally a Byzantine fort, it was built by the Lombard duke of Benevento, Arechi II, in the 8th century and subsequently modified by the Normans and Aragonese, most recently in the 16th century. If you are here during summer, ask the tourist office for a schedule of the annual series of concerts staged here.

Museo Virtuale della Scuola Medica Salernitana
MUSEUM
(☑ 089 257 61 26; www.museovirtualescuolamedica salernitana.beniculturali.it; Via Mercanti 74; adult/reduced €3/1; ⊙ 9.30am-1pm Tue-Wed, 9.30am-1pm & 5-8pm Thu-Sat, 10am-1pm Sun; ⓓ) Slap bang in Salerno's historic centre, this engaging museum deploys 3D and touch-screen technology to explore the teachings and wince-inducing procedures of Salerno's once-famous, now-defunct medical institute. Established around the 9th century, the school was the most important centre of medical knowledge in medieval Europe, reaching the height of its prestige in the 11th century. It was closed in the early 19th century.

Museo Pinacoteca Provinciale
MUSEUM
(☑ 089 258 30 73; www.museibiblioteche.provincia. salerno.it; Via Mercanti 63; adult/reduced €3/1.50; ⊙ 9am-7.45pm Tue-Sun) **FREE** Art enthusiasts should seek out the Museo Pinacoteca Provinciale, located deep in the heart of the historic quarter. Spread throughout six galleries, the museum houses a collection dating from the Renaissance right up to the first half of the 20th century.

🛌 Sleeping

Ostello Ave Gratia Plena
HOSTEL €
(☑ 089 23 47 76; www.ostellodisalerno.it; Via dei Canali; dm/s/d €16/45/65; ⊙year-round; @ 🤖) Housed in a 16th-century convent, Salerno's excellent HI hostel is right in the heart of the *centro storico*. Inside there's a charming central courtyard and a range of bright rooms, from dorms to great bargain doubles with private bathroom. The 2am curfew is for dorms only.

Hotel Montestella
HOTEL €€
(☑ 089 22 51 22; www.hotelmontestella.it; Corso Vittorio Emanuele II 156; s/d/tr €75/100/110; ⊙year-round; ❄ @ 🤖) Within walking distance of just about anywhere worth going to, the Montestella is on Salerno's main pedestrian thoroughfare, halfway between the

centro storico and train station. The rooms are spacious and comfortable, with blue carpeting and patterned wallpaper, while the public spaces have a fresh, modern look. It's one of the best midrange options in town.

🍴 Eating

⭐ Vicolo della Neve
ITALIAN €
(☑ 089 22 57 05; www.vicolodellaneve.it; Vicolo della Neve 24; meals €20; ⊙ 7-11.30pm Thu-Tue) A city institution on a scruffy street, this is the archetypal *centro storico* trattoria, with brick arches, fake frescoes and walls hung with works by local artists. The menu is, similarly, unwaveringly authentic, with pizzas and *calzones, peperoni ripieni* (stuffed peppers) and a top-notch *parmigiana di melanzane* (baked aubergine). It can get incredibly busy: book well in advance.

Pizza Margherita
ITALIAN €
(☑ 089 22 88 80; Corso Garibaldi 201; pizzas/buffet from €5/6.50, lunch menu €8.50; ⊙ 12.30-3.30pm

Temple of Ceres, Paestum (p108)
VIVIDS/GETTY IMAGES ©

Salerno

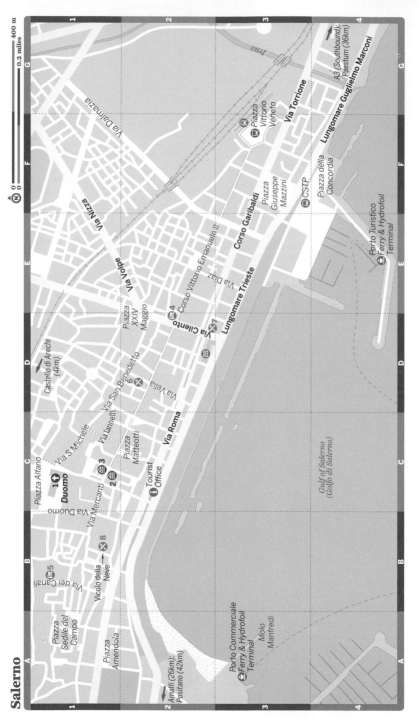

0.2 miles
400 m

G

Castello di Arechi (4km)

Piazza Alfano

1 **Duomo**

Piazza Sedile del Campo

Via del Canali

5

Piazza Amendola

Via Mercanti

Via Duomo

Via S. Michele

Via San Benedetto

8

Vicolo della Neve → Amalfi (26km); Positano (42km) →

Piazza Matteotti

3

2

Tourist Office

Via Iannelli

6

Via Velia

Via Roma

Via Nizza

Via Volpe

Piazza XXIV Maggio

4

Via Cilento

Corso Vittorio Emanuele II

Via Dalmazia

Corso Garibaldi

Via Diaz

7

Lungomare Trieste

Piazza Giuseppe Mazzini

Piazza Vittorio Veneto

Via Torrione

CSTP

Piazza della Concordia

Lungomare Guglielmo Marconi

A3 (Southbound); Paestum (36km) →

Porto Turistico

Ferry & Hydrofoil Terminal

Gulf of Salerno (Golfo di Salerno)

Porto Commerciale Ferry & Hydrofoil Terminal

Molo Manfredi

Salerno

& 7.30pm-midnight; 🖶) It looks like a bland, modern canteen, but this is, in fact, one of Salerno's most popular lunch spots. Locals regularly queue for the lavish lunchtime buffet that, on any given day, might include buffalo mozzarella, salami, mussels in various guises and a range of salads. If that doesn't appeal, the daily lunch menu (pasta, main course, salad and half a litre of bottled water) is chalked up on a blackboard, or there's the regular menu of pizzas, pastas, salads and main courses.

La Cantina del Feudo   ITALIAN €€

(✆ 089 25 46 96; Via Velia 45; meals €28; ◷ noon-2pm & 7-11pm Tue-Sun; ✍) Frequented by locals in the know, this restaurant is tucked up a side street off the pedestrian *corso*. The menu changes daily, but the emphasis is on vegetable dishes like white beans with chicory, noodles and turnip tops, and ravioli stuffed with cheese. The interior has a rural trattoria feel and there's a terrace for alfresco dining.

ⓘ Information

Post Office (Corso Garibaldi 203)
Tourist Office (✆ 089 23 14 32; Lungomare Trieste 7; ◷ 9am-1pm & 3-7pm Mon-Sat) Has limited information.

ⓘ Getting There & Away

CAR & MOTORCYCLE
Salerno is on the A3 between Naples and Reggio di Calabria; the A3 is toll-free from Salerno south. If you want to hire a car, there's a **Europcar** (✆ 089 258 07 75; www.europcar.com; Via Clemente Mauro 18) agency between the train station and Piazza della Concordia.

Paestum

Paestum, or Poseidonia as the city was originally called (in honour of Poseidon, the Greek god of the sea), was founded in the 6th century BC by Greek settlers and fell under Roman control in 273 BC. Decline later set in following the demise of the Roman Empire. Savage raids by the Saracens and periodic outbreaks of malaria forced the steadily dwindling population to abandon the city altogether. Although most people visit Paestum for the day, there is a surprising number of good hotels, and this delightful rural area makes a convenient stopover point for travellers heading for the Cilento region.

🛏 Sleeping

★**Casale Giancesare**   B&B €

(✆0828 72 80 61, 333 1897737; www.casale-gianc esare.it; Via Giancesare 8; s €65-120, d €65-120, apt per week €600-1300; ◷year-round; P✲@🖥🏊) A 19th-century former farmhouse, this elegantly decorated stone-clad B&B is run by the delightful Voza family, who will happily ply you with their homemade wine and *limoncello*. It's located 2.5km from the glories of Paestum and surrounded by vineyards and olive and mulberry trees; views are stunning, particularly from the swimming pool.

★**Hotel Calypso**   HOTEL €€

(✆0828 81 10 31; www.calypsohotel.com; Via Mantegna 63; s €50-75, d €100-150; ◷year-round; P✲@) This is a top choice for artistically or alternatively inclined folk. The large, tastefully decorated rooms have private balconies and some choice handcrafted decor pieces, and a sandy beach is a short stroll away. Owner Roberto is a world traveller who can advise on the local area. Concerts, ranging from folk to classical, are regularly staged during summer.

✕ Eating

Nonna Sceppa   ITALIAN €€

(✆0828 85 10 64; Via Laura 53; meals €35; ◷12.30-3pm & 7.30-11pm Fri-Wed; 🖶) Seek out the superbly prepared, robust dishes at Nonna Sceppa, a family-friendly restaurant that's gaining a reputation throughout the region for excellence. Dishes are firmly seasonal and, during summer, concentrate on fresh seafood like the refreshingly simple grilled fish with lemon. Other popular choices include risotto with zucchini and artichokes, and spaghetti with lobster.

PAESTUM'S TEMPLES

Paestum's Temples (☑ 0828 81 10 23; incl museum adult/reduced €10/5; ⊘ 8.45am-7.45pm, last entry 7pm Jun & Jul, as early as 3.35pm Nov) A Unesco World Heritage Site, these temples are among the best-preserved monuments of Magna Graecia, the Greek colony that once covered much of southern Italy. Rediscovered in the late 18th century, the site as a whole wasn't unearthed until the 1950s. Lacking the tourist mobs that can sully better-known archaeological sites, the place has a wonderful serenity. Take sandwiches and prepare to stay at least three hours. In spring the temples are particularly stunning, surrounded by scarlet poppies.

Buy your tickets in the museum, just east of the site, before entering from the main entrance on the northern end. The first structure is the 6th-century-BC **Tempio di Cerere** (Temple of Ceres); originally dedicated to Athena, it served as a Christian church in medieval times.

As you head south, you can pick out the basic outline of the large rectangular forum, the heart of the ancient city. Among the partially standing buildings are the vast domestic housing area and, further south, the amphitheatre; both provide evocative glimpses of daily life here in Roman times. In the former houses you'll see mosaic floors, and a marble *impluvium* that stood in the atrium and collected rainwater.

The **Tempio di Nettuno** (Temple of Neptune), dating from about 450 BC, is the largest and best preserved of the three temples at Paestum; only parts of its inside walls and roof are missing. Almost next door, the so-called **basilica** (in fact, a temple to the goddess Hera) is Paestum's oldest-surviving monument. Dating from the middle of the 6th century BC, it's a magnificent sight, with nine columns across and 18 along the sides. Ask someone to take your photo next to one of the columns: it's a good way to appreciate the scale.

Save time for the **museum** (☑ 0828 81 10 23; ⊘ 8.30am-7.30pm, last entry 6.45pm, closed 1st & 3rd Mon of month), which covers two floors and houses a collection of fascinating, if weathered, metopes (bas-relief friezes). This collection includes 33 of the original 36 metopes from the Tempio di Argiva Hera (Temple of Argive Hera), situated 9km north of Paestum, of which virtually nothing else remains. The star exhibit is the 5th-century-BC fresco Tomba del Truffatore (Tomb of the Diver), thought to represent the passage from life to death with its frescoed depiction of a diver in mid air. The fresco was discovered in 1968 inside the lid of the tomb of a young man, alongside his drinking cup and oil flasks, which he would perhaps have used to oil himself for wrestling matches. Rare for the period in that it shows a human form, the fresco expresses pure delight in physicality, its freshness and grace eternally arresting. Below the diver, a symposium of men repose languidly on low couches and brandish drinking cups.

ⓘ Information

Tourist Office (☑ 0828 81 10 16; www.infopaestum.it; Via Magna Crecia 887; ⊘ 9am-1.30pm & 2.30-7pm Mon-Sat)

Agropoli

POP 20,700

Located just south of Paestum, Agropoli is a busy summer resort but otherwise a pleasant, tranquil town that makes a good base for exploring the Cilento coastline.

The town has been inhabited since Neolithic times, with subsequent inhabitants including the Greeks, the Romans, the Byzantines and the Saracens. In 915 Agropoli fell under the jurisdiction of the bishops and was subsequently ruled by feudal lords. It was a target of raids from North Africa in the 16th and 17th centuries, when the population dwindled to just a few hundred. Today its residents number closer to 20,000, making it the largest (and most vibrant) town along the Cilento coast.

⊙ Sights & Activities

To reach the *centro storico*, head for Piazza Veneto Victoria, the pedestrian-only part of the modern town, where cafes and gelaterie are interspersed with plenty of shopping choice. Head up Corso Garibaldi and take the wide Ennio Balbo Scaloni steps until you reach the fortified *borgo* (medieval town). Follow the signs to the castle. The town is famed for its pristine, golden, sandy beaches.

Il Castello
CASTLE

(⊙10am-8pm) **FREE** Built by the Byzantines in the 5th century, the castle was strengthened during the Angevin period, the time of the Vespro War bloodbath. It continued to be modified, and only part of the original defensive wall remains. It's an enjoyable walk here through the historic centre, and you can wander the ramparts and enjoy magnificent views of the coastline and town. Not just a tourist sight, the castle is utilised by the locals: there's a permanent gallery showcasing the work of contemporary artists and a small open-air auditorium where summer concerts take place.

Cilento Sub Diving Center
DIVING

(☑338 2374603; www.cilentosub.com; Via San Francesco 30; single dives from €35; ⛵) Indulge in your favourite watery pursuit here. Courses include snorkelling for beginners, open-water junior dives (from 12 years) and wreck diving; the latter includes the harrowing (for some) viewing of the hulks of ships, tanks and planes that were famously destroyed in the region during WWII. Diving sites include such tantalising areas as the waters off the coast at Paestum, where – who knows? – you may just come across your very own bronze Apollo.

🛌 Sleeping

Anna
B&B, APARTMENT €

(☑0974 82 37 63; www.bbanna.it; Via S Marco 28-30, Agropoli; d €75-90; ⊙year-round; **P**❄) A great location, across from the town's sweeping sandy beach, this trim budget choice is known locally for its restaurant, where you can salivate over homemade morning *cornetti*. The rooms are large and plain with small balconies; specify a sea view to enjoy the sun setting over Sorrento. Sunbeds and bicycles can be hired for a minimal price.

La Lanterna
AGRITURISMO €

(☑089 79 02 51; www.cilento.it/lanterna; Via della Lanterna 8, Agropoli; dm €16, d €34-45, tr €51-55, q €68-72; ⊙Easter-Oct; **P**@) Ivo and Tiziana are great hosts at this friendly place, 1km from the centre. The homey cabin accommodation is great value, set in the large terraced gardens. Dorms are clean with lockers, while the communal breakfast of rolls with cream cheese or jam and homemade cake is better than most. Internet €3 per hour.

🍴 Eating

⭐ Anna
PIZZA €

(☑0974 82 37 63; www.ristorantepizzeriaanna.it; Lungomare San Marco 32; pizzas/meals from €4/15;

⊙11am-midnight) At the city-centre end of the promenade, this has been a locals' favourite for decades. Family-run, with a small B&B upstairs, Anna is best known for its pizzas, especially since a British broadsheet named Anna's *sorpresa* the best pizza in Italy in 2010. Its seven-slice selection includes mussels, aubergines, zucchini, marinated pork, ham, prawns and spicy sausage. More traditional seafood dishes include grilled swordfish. This is also a good place for an energy-stoking start to the day, with more than eight types of *cornetti* (croissants) to choose from.

Bar Gelateria del Corso
GELATERIA €

(Corso Garibaldi 22-24; cakes/ice creams from €1.50/2, cocktails from €2.50; ⊙8am-9pm) The most popular spot for slurping an ice cream, sipping a cocktail or salivating over a cream cake. Wicker chairs are positioned for people-watching on this pedestrian shopping street. There are some unusual ice-cream flavours, including *marron glacé* (candied chestnut) and *limone sicilia* (Sicilian lemon), plus yoghurt-based choices such as *frutti di bosco* (fruit of the forest).

Il Gambero
SEAFOOD €€

(☑0974 82 28 94; www.gambero.it; Via Lungomare San Marco 234; meals from €25; ⊙12.15-3.30pm & 7pm-midnight, closed Tue winter) Il Gambero is located across from Agropoli's long sandy beach – get here early to grab a table out front and enjoy the sun setting over Sorrento with Capri twinkling in the distance. Specialities include seafood mixed salad, pasta with clams and pumpkin, and fried mixed fish. Although there are some non-seafood dishes, the fish has star billing. Reservations recommended.

ℹ Information

Tourist Office (☑0974 82 74 71; Viale Europa 34; ⊙9.30am-2pm) Not a lot of information, but can provide a basic city map.

ℹ Getting There & Around

There's a **car-rental outfit** (☑0974 82 80 99; Via A De Gasperi 82; per day from €50).

Cilento Coast

While the Cilento stretch of coastline lacks the gloss and sophistication of the Amalfi Coast, it can afford to have a slight air of superiority when it comes to its beaches: a combination of secluded coves and long stretches

Santa Maria di Castellabate beach

of golden sand with a welcome lack of over-priced ice creams and sunbeds. Beyond the options outlined below, the far-southeastern stop along the coastline is Sapri, which has two pleasant beaches in the centre of town.

Agropoli to Castellabate

Around 14km south of Agropoli is the for-mer fishing village of Santa Maria di Cas-tellabate. Santa Maria's golden sandy beach stretches for around 4km, which equals plenty of towel space on the sand, even in midsummer.

Approached from its coastal sidekick, Santa Maria de Castellabate, the summit of Castellabate is marked by the broad Belve-dere di San Costabile, from where there are sweeping coastal views. Flanking this are the shell of a 12th-century castle, with only the defensive walls still standing, and an art gal-lery. The surrounding labyrinth of narrow pedestrian streets is punctuated by ancient archways, small piazzas and the occasional *palazzo* (mansion). The animated heart and soul of town is the numerological mouthful Piazza 10 Ottobre 1123, with its panoramic views of the Valle dell'Annunziata.

San Marco di Castellabate to Acciaroli

Heading south from Castellabate, the next stop is the pretty little harbour at San Marco di Castellabate, overlooked by the handsome, ivy-clad Approdo hotel. This was once an important Greek and Roman port, and tombs and other relics have been discovered that are now on view in the mu-seum at Paestum. The area between Santa Maria di Castellabate and San Marco is pop-ular for diving: contact Galatea (☑ 0974 96 67 07, 334 3485643; single dives from €45). San Marco's blue-flag beach is a continuation of the sandy stretch from Santa Maria di Castellabate.

The coastal road heading south lacks the drama (views *and* traffic) of its Amalfi coun-terpart but is still prettily panoramic. It's an area that Ernest Hemingway apparently rated highly, particularly Acciaroli, which – despite the disquieting amount of surround-ing concrete – has a charming centre. Head for the sea and the peeling facade of the Par-rocchia di Acciaroli church, with its abstract 1920s stained-glass windows. The surround-ing streets and piazzas have been tastefully restored using local stone and traditional architecture, and the cafes, bars and restau-rants have a buzzing, fashionable appeal.

Pioppi to Pisciotta

A short 10km hop south of Acciaroli is tiny picturesque Pioppi, with its pristine, pebble beach and handful of shops and restaurants.

Next stop is Marina di Casal Velino, which features a small, pretty harbour and a family-style stretch of sand, complete with plenty of ice-cream opportunities, a playground and pedal boats.

Continuing southeast, Ascea – best known as the home of philosophers Parmenides and Zeno of Elea, as well as the famous Eleatic School of Philosophy – boasts some impressive Greek ruins. Fronted by 5km of glorious sandy beach, the town is wonderful for a dip.

Further on, lovely Pisciotta is a medieval town piled high above a ridge. Head straight for the central Piazza Raffaele Pinto, its terraced bars and benches occupied by robust elderly locals. There are a couple of excellent restaurants in town and one of the region's top boutique hotels. Be sure to stop by the Marina di Pisciotta, lined with seafood restaurants and cafes. Carry on to the far end of the promenade and take a look at the stones and pebbles on the beach, fabulously patterned and in all shades of mauve, grey, cream and ochre.

◉ Sights & Activities

Velia   ARCHAEOLOGICAL SITE
See p48

🛏 Sleeping

★ Marulivo Hotel   BOUTIQUE HOTEL €
(✆ 0974 973 792; www.marulivohotel.it; Via Castello, Pisciotta; d €85-100; ☺ Easter-Oct; ❄ 🛜) Great for romance, or just a stress-free break in idyllic surroundings. Located in the narrow web of lanes behind medieval Pisciotta's main piazza, rooms feature earthy colours, antique furnishings, crisp white linen and exposed stone walls. The rooftop terrace with sea views and an adjacent small bar is unbeatable for lingering over a cold drink.

Raggio di Sole   AGRITURISMO €
(✆ 0974 96 73 56; www.agriturismoraggiodisole.it; Via Terrate, Castellabate; d €80; ☺ Apr-Nov; P ❄) Situated on the outskirts of town coming from Santa Maria di Castellabate, this welcoming *agriturismo* is just one mountain peak away from the town, so the views are superb, with the sea and the island of Capri beyond. The 200-year-old farmhouse has been thoroughly updated, and rooms are plain and modern with balconies. The main house is surrounded by greenery, including lofty eucalyptus, citrus and olive trees, while below there is a small farmyard.

Villa Sirio   HOTEL €€
(✆ 0974 96 01 62; www.villasirio.it; Via Lungomare de Simone 15, Santa Maria di Castellabate; d €130-220; ☺ Apr-Nov; P ❄) Dating from 1912, this family-owned hotel has a classic, elegant facade with ochre paintwork and traditional green shutters. The rooms are brightly furnished with a yellow, blue and turquoise colour scheme; shiny marble-clad bathrooms come complete with hot tub. The small balconies have forfeited the plastic for tasteful marble tables and have seamless sea views with Capri in the distance.

🍴 Eating

Arlecchino   SEAFOOD €
(✆ 0974 96 18 89; Via Guglielmini, Santa Maria di Castellabate; pizzas from €4, meals €20; ☺ noon-2.30pm & 7-11pm Mar-Nov; 🎎) Located across from the beach in the pretty southernmost part of Santa Maria, popular Arlecchino has picture windows overlooking the small sweep of sand. Packed to the gills at weekends, the restaurant primarily offers seafood, including a recommended *sepia alla griglia* (grilled cuttlefish). Finish with the calorific delight of local speciality *torta ricotta e pera* (ricotta and pear tart).

Il Capriccio   ITALIAN €
(✆ 0974 84 52 41; Corso da Spiafriddo, Castellabate; meals €18) On the road to Perdifumo, this is a favourite local choice. An unassuming place with a terrace, Il Capriccio has a gracious host in owner Enxo. The menu runs the gamut from seafood classics such as *zuppa di cozze* (mussel soup) and *pollpetti affogati* (poached octopus) to less fishy options such as *zuppa di ceci* (chickpea soup). The *crostata della nonna* (grandma's cake) is as promising as it sounds: a delicious confection of puff pastry, almonds and seasonal fruit.

Pizza in Piazza   PIZZA €
(✆ 320 0966325; Piazza Vittorio Emanuele, Acciaroli; pizzas from €4; ☺ Apr-Nov; 🎎) An upper-crust pizza place on a pretty piazza with magnificent rubber trees and wisteria-draped walls. Sit outside or eat on the go. The pizzas include all the standard choices but are excellent, with a crispy base and garden-fresh ingredients. The *caprese* (€7) comes particularly recommended, with its simple topping of cherry tomatoes, *mozzarella di bufala* and basil leaves.

THE MEDITERRANEAN DIET

Pioppi has the right to feel smug: based on initial observations of the town in the late 1950s, American medical researcher Dr Ancel Keys launched his famous study concerning the health benefits of the Mediterranean diet. Of the residents of Pioppi, Keys famously wrote: 'The people were older and vigorous. They were walking up and down the hillside collecting wild grains, and were out fishing before sun-up and going out again in the late afternoon and rowing boats'.

Keys was struck by the low rate of heart disease among poor people here, compared to the rate among well-fed northern Europeans and Americans. He himself adopted the Mediterranean-style diet and lived to be 101 years old. Ironically, you have to be rich to eat healthy foods like a peasant these days, with virgin olive oil, fresh fish and organic fruit and vegetables generally costing far more than processed foods.

Join today's elderly Pioppi residents in their more leisurely pursuit of dozing on the shady benches in lovely Piazza de Millenario with its handy central bar. Then, suitably rested, take a healthy Med-diet picnic to the beach a few steps away.

★ I Tre Gufi   ITALIAN €€

(☑ 0974 97 30 42; Via Roma, Pisciotta; meals €25; ⊙ noon-3pm & 7-11pm) Follow the signs from Pisciotta's sweeping Piazza Raffaele Pinto to this restaurant in a star setting, its long, wide terrace overlooking the pine-forested hillside stretching down to the sea. The menu has plenty of choice, with seafood the speciality. There's also a good choice of salads, plus pasta, *fagiolini* (green beans), risotto and specials like sea bass with porcini mushrooms and olives. The dining room is lined with jazzy abstract paintings, and there's an adjacent cafe and gelateria (they make their own ice cream).

Cantina Belvedere   ITALIAN €€

(☑ 0974 96 70 30; www.cantinabelvedere.it; Castellabate; meals €30; ⊙ noon-2.30pm & 7-11.30pm Wed-Mon) East of the castle, this restaurant clings limpetlike to the vertiginous cliff, guaranteeing uninterrupted sea views. When you're not gazing at the view, you can enjoy octopus carpaccio, peppered fillet steak or one of the plentiful pasta and pizza choices. This is a popular spot for wedding parties, so be sure to reserve ahead.

🍸 Drinking & Nightlife

Il Ciclope   CLUB

(☑ 0974 93 03 18; www.ilciclope.com; Marina di Camerota) While the Cilento region may not be well known to your average tourist, it is definitely on the map when it comes to clubbing. An impressive array of big-name DJs have spun their stuff at the club, which occupies four limestone caves.

Palinuro

POP 4800

Palinuro is located in a picturesque bay sheltered by a promontory. Note that the majority of hotels and restaurants are seasonal and are only open from Easter to October.

◉ Sights & Activities

Aside from the grottoes, Palinuro is famous for its beaches. For a quiet cove, head south of town to Spiaggia Marmelli, surrounded by lush banks of greenery. The beach is approached via steep steps, and there's a small car park at the top. The town's main beach is Spiaggia Palinuro, which stretches for around 4km north of the centre. Palinuro's postcard-pretty harbour has colourful fishing boats, several bars and a wide swath of sand.

Grotta Azzurra   GROTTO

(Palinuro) Although it doesn't have the hype of its Capri counterpart, Palinuro's Grotta Azzurra (Blue Grotto) is similarly spectacular, with a Technicolour play of light and hue. It owes its name to the extraordinary effect produced by the sunlight that filters inside from an underground passage lying at a depth of about 8m. The best time to visit is the afternoon, due to the position of the sun.

Da Alessandro   BOATING

(☑ 347 654 09 31; www.costieradelcilento.it; trips from €15) Da Alessandro, at a kiosk at the harbour, runs trips to Palinuro's Grotta Azzurra as well as four other caves in the area.

🛏 Sleeping

Antico Maniero Palinuro B&B €€
(☑0974 93 30 38; www.anticomanieropalinuro.it; Colle San Sergio, Centola; d €110; ⊙Easter-Oct) Located in a stone mansion with a gorgeous terrace and sweeping sea views, Antico Maniero Palinuro features unashamedly romantic rooms – with drapes, lace bedspreads and dark wood furniture – that stay on the right side of kitsch. Located between Centola and Palinuro, it's a good option if you're driving around the Cilento or along the coast.

Albergo Santa Caterina HOTEL €€
(☑0974 93 10 19; www.albergosantacaterina.com; Via Indipendenza 53, Palinuro; d €100-155; ⊙Easter-Oct; P🗙@🛜) At this superb hotel on the main street, guestroom colour schemes vary from brilliant canary yellow to deep Mediterranean blue. All have good-size bathrooms, with tubs as well as showers, and private terraces. Sea views cost €20 more. The satellite TV here is a rare treat in these parts: great if you are suffering from international-news withdrawal.

🗙 Eating

Pasticceria Egidio PASTRIES €
(☑0974 93 14 60; Via Santa Maria 15; sfogliatelle €1.50; ⊙9am-8pm) Run by the reassuringly plump Egidio family, this *pasticceria* has a cake display backed by a large bakery where breads (including *integrale*) arrive steaming hot for picnic time. The cakes really are as good as they look: *sfogliatelle* filled with fresh ricotta, *frollini* (mini fruit and chocolate tarts) and the all-time favourite, crumbly *amaretti* (macaroons).

Bar Da Siena GELATERIA €
(☑0974 93 10 19; Via Indipendenza 53; ice creams from €1.50; ⊙8am-9pm; 🖐) Part of the Albergo Santa Caterina, this L-shaped bar (cocktails from €3) serves the best ice cream in town with *semi freddi* (semi cold) and yoghurt-based ices, as well as enticing flavours such as *ricotta e pistacchio* (ricotta and pistachio) and the possibly less appealing *zuppa inglese* (literally 'English soup': trifle). The romantic terrace is perfect for a little locked-eyes-over-ice-cream time.

⭐ Ristorante Core a Core ITALIAN €€
(☑0974 93 16 91; www.coreacorepalinuro.it; Via Piano Faracchio 13; meals €30; ⊙noon-3pm & 7-11pm) Ignore the cheesy heart-shaped sign: with its glorious garden setting and great reputation for seafood, Core a Core is your best bet in Palinuro. The *antipasti al mare* (€19.50) is superb, and there's a menu of proper kids food. Book in advance – it's popular.

Ristorante Miramare SEAFOOD €€
(☑0974 93 09 70; www.miramarepalinuro.it; Corso Pisacane 89; meals from €28; ⊙noon-3pm & 7-11.30pm) Enjoying a supreme position, with a broad terrace overlooking the turquoise sea and small adjacent sandy cove, this place is part of the same-name hotel. The menu is predominantly seafood based and holds few surprises, although there is the odd nod to the international palate, including roast beef. Otherwise, *spaghetti alla vongole* (spaghetti with clams) is a safe bet.

🍷 Drinking & Nightlife

Babylon BAR
(☑0974 93 14 56; www.babylonpalinuro.it; Via Porto 47; cocktails €5; ⊙8am-midnight) A welcome addition to Palinuro's bar scene. The sprawling terrace with perspex furniture and palms creates a glamorous space for live music every Saturday in summer.

ℹ Information

Tourist Office (☑0974 93 81 44; Piazza Virgilio; ⊙9.30am-1.30pm & 5-7pm Mon-Sat, 9.30am-1.30pm Sun) Can provide a town map and general information.

Great Window at Cape Palinuro
KONRAD WOTHE/LOOK-FOTO/GETTY IMAGES

ROAD TRIP ESSENTIALS

Italy
Driving Guide

Italy's stunning natural scenery, comprehensive road network and passion for cars make it a wonderful road-trip destination.

Driving Fast Facts

Right or left? Drive on the right

Manual or automatic? Mostly manual

Legal driving age 18

Top speed limit 130km/h to 150km/h (on autostradas)

Signature car Flaming red Ferrari or Fiat 500

DRIVING LICENCE & DOCUMENTS

When driving in Italy you are required to carry with you:

➡ The vehicle registration document

➡ Your driving licence

➡ Proof of third-party liability insurance

Driving Licence

➡ All EU member states' driving licences are fully recognised throughout Europe.

➡ Travellers from other countries should obtain an International Driving Permit (IDP) through their national automobile association. This should be carried with your licence; it is not a substitute for it.

➡ No licence is needed to ride a scooter under 50cc. To ride a motorcycle or scooter up to 125cc, you'll need a licence (a car licence will do). For motorcycles over 125cc you need a motorcycle licence.

INSURANCE

➡ Third-party liability insurance is mandatory for all vehicles in Italy, including cars brought in from abroad.

➡ If driving an EU-registered vehicle, your home country insurance is sufficient. Ask your insurer for a European Accident Statement (EAS) form, which can simplify matters in the event of an accident.

➡ Hire agencies provide the minimum legal insurance, but you can supplement it if you choose.

HIRING A CAR

Car-hire agencies are widespread in Italy but pre-booking on the internet is often cheaper. Considerations before renting:

➡ Bear in mind that a car is generally more hassle than it's worth in cities, so only hire one for the time you'll be on the open road.

➡ Consider vehicle size carefully. High fuel prices, extremely narrow streets and tight parking conditions mean that smaller is often better.

➡ Road signs can be iffy in remote areas, so consider booking and paying for satnav.

Standard regulations:

➡ Many agencies have a minimum rental age of 25 and a maximum of 79. You can sometimes hire if you're over 21 but supplementary costs will apply.

Local Expert: Driving Tips

A representative of the Automobile Club d'Italia (ACI) offers these pearls to ease your way on Italian roads:

➡ Pay particular attention to the weather. In summer when it gets very hot, always carry a bottle of water with you and have some fresh fruit to eat. Italy is a sunny country but, in winter, watch out for ice, snow and fog.

➡ On the extra-urban roads and autostradas, cars have to have their headlights on even during the day.

➡ Watch out for signs at the autostrada toll booths – the lanes marked 'Telepass' are for cars that pay through an automatic electronic system without stopping.

➡ Watch out in the cities – big and small – for the Limited Traffic Zones (ZTL) and pay parking. There is no universal system for indicating these or their hours.

➡ To rent you'll need a credit card, valid driver's licence (with IDP if necessary) and passport or photo ID. Note that some companies require that you've had your licence for at least a year.

➡ Hire cars come with the minimum legal insurance, which you can supplement by purchasing additional coverage.

➡ Check with your credit-card company to see if it offers a Collision Damage Waiver, which covers you for additional damage if you use that card to pay for the car.

The following are among the most competitive multinational and Italian car-hire agencies.

Avis (☑199 100133; www.avis.com)
Budget (☑800 4723325; www.budget.com)
Europcar (☑199 307030; www.europcar.com)
Hertz (☑199 112211; www.hertz.com)

Italy by Car (☑091 6393120; www.italyby car.it) Partners with Thrifty.
Maggiore (☑199 151120; www.maggiore.it) Partners with Alamo and National.

Motorcycles

Agencies throughout Italy rent motorbikes, ranging from small Vespas to larger touring bikes. Prices start at around €80/400 per day/week for a 650cc motorcycle.

BRINGING YOUR OWN VEHICLE

There are no major obstacles to driving your own vehicle into Italy. But you will have to adjust your car's headlights if it's a left-hand-drive UK model. You'll need to carry the following in the car:

➡ A warning triangle

➡ A fluorescent reflective vest to wear if you have to stop on a major road

➡ Snow chains if travelling in mountainous areas between 15 October and 15 April

MAPS

We recommend you purchase a good road map for your trip. The best driving maps are produced by the **Touring Club Italiano** (www.touringclub.com), Italy's largest map publisher. They are available at bookstores across Italy or online at the following:

Stanfords (www.stanfords.co.uk)
Omni Resources (www.omnimap.com)

Italy Playlist

Nessun Dorma Puccini

O sole mio Traditional

Tu vuoi fare l'americano Renato Carsone

Vieni via con me Paolo Conte

That's Amore Dean Martin

Four Seasons Vivaldi

ROADS & CONDITIONS

Italy's extensive road network covers the entire peninsula and with enough patience you'll be able to get just about anywhere. Road quality varies – the autostradas are generally excellent but smaller roads, particularly in rural areas, are not always great. Heavy rain can cause axle-busting potholes to form and road surfaces to crumble.

Traffic in and around the main cities is bad during morning and evening rush hours. Coastal roads get very busy on summer weekends. As a rule, traffic is quietest between 2pm and 4pm.

Road Categories

Autostradas Italy boasts an extensive network of autostradas, represented on road signs by a white 'A' followed by a number on a green background. The main north–south link is the Autostrada del Sole (the 'Motorway of the Sun'), which runs from Milan (Milano) to Reggio di Calabria. It's called the A1 from Milan to Rome (Roma), the A2 from Rome to Naples (Napoli), and the A3 from Naples to Reggio di Calabria. There are tolls on most motorways, payable by cash or credit card as you exit. To calculate the toll price for any given journey, use the route planner on www.autostrade.it.

Strade statali State highways; represented on maps by 'S' or 'SS'. Vary from four-lane highways to two-lane main roads. The latter can be extremely slow, especially in mountainous regions.

Strade regionali Regional highways connecting small villages. Coded 'SR' or 'R'.

Strade provinciali Provincial highways; coded 'SP' or 'P'.

Strade locali Often not even paved or mapped.

Along with their A or SS number, some Italian roads are labelled with an E number – for example, the A4 autostrada is also shown as the E64 on maps and signs. This E number refers to the road's designation on the Europe-wide E-road network. E routes, which often cross national boundaries, are generally made up of major national roads strung together. The E70, for example, traverses 10 countries and includes the Italian A4, A21 and A32 autostradas, as it runs from northern Spain to Georgia.

Limited Traffic Zones

Many town and city centres are off-limits to unauthorised traffic at certain times. If you drive past a sign with the wording *Zona a Traffico Limitato* you are entering a Limited Traffic Zone (ZTL) and risk being caught on camera and fined. Being in a hire car will not exempt you from this rule.

If you think your hotel might be in a ZTL, contact them beforehand to ask about access arrangements.

ROAD RULES

➡ Drive on the right side of the road and overtake on the left. Unless otherwise indicated, give way to cars entering an intersection from a road on your right.

➡ Seatbelt use (front and rear) is required by law; violators are subject to an on-the-spot fine.

➡ In the event of a breakdown, a warning triangle is compulsory, as is use of an approved yellow or orange safety vest if you leave your vehicle. Recommended accessories include a first-aid kit, spare-bulb kit and fire extinguisher.

➡ Italy's blood-alcohol limit is 0.05%, and random breath tests take place. If you're involved in an accident while under the influence, the penalties can be severe.

Road-Trip Websites

AUTOMOBILE ASSOCIATIONS

Automobile Club d'Italia (www. aci.it) Has a comprehensive online guide to motoring in Italy. Provides 24-hour roadside assistance.

CONDITIONS & TRAFFIC

Autostrade (www.autostrade.it) Route planner, weather forecasts and the traffic situation in real time. Also lists service stations, petrol prices and toll costs.

MAPS

Michelin (www.viamichelin.it) Online road-trip planner.

Tutto Città (www.tuttocitta.it) Good for detailed town and city maps.

Driving Problem-Buster

I can't speak Italian, will that be a problem? When at a petrol station you might have to ask the attendant for your fill-up. The thing to do here is ask for the amount you want, so *venti euro* for €20 or *pieno* for full. And always specify *benzina senza piombo* for unleaded petrol and *gasolio* for diesel. At autostrada toll booths, the amount you owe appears on a read-out by the booth.

What should I do if my car breaks down? Call the service number of your car-hire company. The Automobile Club d'Italia (ACI) provides a 24-hour roadside emergency service – call ☎803 116 from a landline or mobile with an Italian provider or ☎800 116800 from a foreign mobile phone. Foreigners do not have to join but instead pay a per-incident fee. Note that in the event of a breakdown, a warning triangle is compulsory, as is use of an approved yellow or orange safety vest if you leave your vehicle.

What if I have an accident? For minor accidents there's no need to call the police. Fill in an accident report – Constatazione Amichevole di Incidente (CAI; Agreed Motor Accident Statement) – through your car-hire firm or insurance company.

What should I do if I get stopped by the police? The police will want to see your passport (or photo ID), licence, car registration papers and proof of insurance.

What if I can't find anywhere to stay? Always book ahead in summer and popular holiday periods. Italy doesn't have chains of roadside motels so if it's getting late head to the nearest town and look for signs for an *albergo* (hotel).

Will I be able to find ATMs? Some autostrada service stations have ATMs (known as *bancomat* in Italian). Otherwise, they are widely available in towns and cities.

Will I need to pay tolls in advance? No. When you join an autostrada you have to pick up a ticket at the barrier. When you exit you pay based on the distance you've covered. Pay by cash or credit card. Avoid Telepass lanes at toll stations.

Are the road signs easy to read? Most signs are fairly obvious but it helps to know that town/city centres are indicated by the word *centro* and a kind of black-and-white bullseye sign; *divieto fermata* means 'no stopping'; and *tutte le direzione* means 'all directions', i.e access to major roads or intersections.

➡ Headlights are compulsory day and night for all vehicles on autostradas and main roads.

➡ Helmets are required on all two-wheeled transport.

➡ Motorbikes can enter most restricted traffic areas in Italian cities.

➡ Speeding fines follow EU standards and are proportionate with the number of kilometres that you are caught driving over the speed limit, reaching up to €2000 with possible suspension of your driving licence. Speed limits are as follows:

Autostradas 130km/h to 150km/h
Other main highways 110km/h

Minor, non-urban roads 90km/h
Built-up areas 50km/h

Road Etiquette

➡ Italian drivers are fast, aggressive and skilful. Lane hopping and late braking are the norm and it's not uncommon to see cars tailgating at 130km/h. Don't expect cars to slow down for you or let you out. As soon as you see a gap, go for it. Italians expect the unexpected and react swiftly, but they're not used to ditherers, so be decisive.

➡ Flashing is common on the roads and has several meanings. If a car behind you flashes it means: 'Get out of the way' or 'Don't pull out, I'm not stopping'. But if an approaching car flashes you, it's warning you that there's a police check ahead.

➡ Use of the car horn is widespread. It might be a warning but it might equally be an expression of frustration at slow-moving traffic or celebration that the traffic light's turning green.

Coins

Always try to keep some coins to hand. They come in very useful for parking meters.

PARKING

➡ Parking is a major headache. Space is at a premium in towns and cities and Italy's traffic wardens are annoyingly efficient.

➡ Parking spaces outlined in blue are designated for paid parking – get a ticket from the nearest meter (coins only) or *tabaccaio* (tobacconist) and display it on your dashboard. Note, however, that charges often don't apply overnight, typically between 8pm and 8am.

➡ White or yellow lines almost always indicate that residential permits are needed.

➡ Traffic police generally turn a blind eye to motorcycles or scooters parked on footpaths.

FUEL

➡ You'll find filling stations all over, but smaller ones tend to close between about 1pm and 3.30pm and on Sunday afternoons.

➡ Many have *fai da te* (self-service) pumps that you can use any time. Simply insert a bank note into the payment machine and press the number of the pump you want.

➡ Italy's petrol prices are among the highest in Europe and vary from one service station (*benzinaio, stazione di servizio*) to another. When this book was researched, lead-free petrol (*benzina senza piombo*) averaged €1.63 per litre, with diesel (*gasolio*) averaging €1.35 per litre.

Road Distances (km)

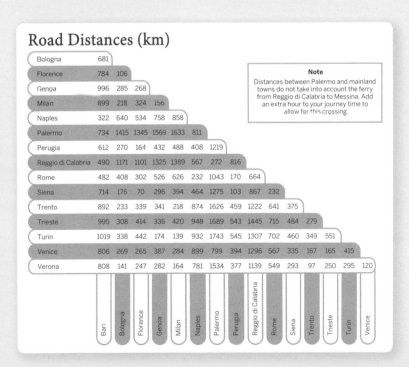

	Bari	Bologna	Florence	Genoa	Milan	Naples	Palermo	Perugia	Reggio di Calabria	Rome	Siena	Trento	Trieste	Turin	Venice
Bologna	681														
Florence	784	106													
Genoa	996	285	268												
Milan	899	218	324	156											
Naples	322	640	534	758	858										
Palermo	734	1415	1345	1569	1633	811									
Perugia	612	270	164	432	488	408	1219								
Reggio di Calabria	490	1171	1101	1325	1389	567	272	816							
Rome	482	408	302	526	626	232	1043	170	664						
Siena	714	176	70	296	394	464	1275	103	867	232					
Trento	892	233	339	341	218	874	1626	459	1222	641	375				
Trieste	995	308	414	336	420	948	1689	543	1445	715	484	279			
Turin	1019	338	442	174	139	932	1743	545	1307	702	460	349	551		
Venice	806	269	265	387	284	899	799	394	1296	567	335	167	165	415	
Verona	808	141	247	282	164	781	1534	377	1139	549	293	97	250	295	120

Note
Distances between Palermo and mainland towns do not take into account the ferry from Reggio di Calabria to Messina. Add an extra hour to your journey time to allow for this crossing.

The Blue Ribbon Drive

Originally designed for horse-drawn carriages, the SS163, nicknamed the Nastro Azzurro (Blue Ribbon), tends to become even narrower on hairpin bends. To avoid blocking oncoming buses, check the circular mirrors on the roadside and listen for the sound of klaxons – if you hear one, slow right down as it will invariably be followed by a coach. Avoid peak season (July and August) and morning, lunchtime and evening rush hours. The trick to driving the coast is to stay calm, even when your toddler throws up all over the back seat or your partner tells you to look at the view while you're inching around a blind corner.

SAFETY

The main safety threat to motorists is theft. Hire cars and foreign vehicles are a target for robbers and although you're unlikely to have a problem, thefts do occur. As a general rule, always lock your car and never leave anything showing, particularly valuables, and certainly not overnight. If at all possible, avoid leaving luggage in an unattended car. It's a good idea to pay extra to leave your car in supervised car parks.

RADIO

RAI, Italy's state broadcaster, operates three national radio stations – Radio 1, 2 and 3 – offering news, current affairs, classical and commercial music, and endless phone-ins. Isoradio, another RAI station, provides regular news and traffic bulletins. There are also thousands of commercial radio stations, many broadcasting locally. Major ones include Radio Capital, good for modern hits; Radio Deejay, aimed at a younger audience; and Radio 24, which airs news and talk shows.

Italy
Travel Guide

GETTING THERE & AWAY

AIR

Italy's main international airports:

Rome Leonardo da Vinci (Fiumicino; www.adr.it) Italy's principal airport.

Rome Ciampino (www.adr.it) Hub for Ryanair flights to Rome (Roma).

Milan Malpensa (www.milanomalpensa1.eu, www.milanomalpensa2.eu) Main airport of Milan (Milano).

Milan Linate (www.milanolinate.eu) Milan's second airport.

Bergamo Orio al Serio (www.sacbo.it)

Turin (www.turin-airport.com)

Bologna Guglielmo Marconi (www.bologna-airport.it)

Pisa Galileo Galilei (www.pisa-airport.com) Main international airport for Tuscany.

Venice Marco Polo (www.veniceairport.it)

Naples Capodichino (www.gesac.it)

Bari Palese (www.aeroportidipuglia.it)

Catania Fontanarossa (www.aeroporto.catania.it) Sicily's busiest airport.

Palermo Falcone-Borsellino (www.gesap.it)

Cagliari Elmas (www.sogaer.it) Main gateway for Sardinia.

Car hire is available at all of these airports.

CAR & MOTORCYCLE

Driving into Italy is fairly straightforward – thanks to the Schengen Agreement, there are no customs checks when driving in from neighbours France, Switzerland, Austria and Slovenia.

Aside from the coast roads linking Italy with France and Slovenia, border crossings into Italy mostly involve tunnels through the Alps (open year-round) or mountain passes (seasonally closed or requiring snow chains). The list below outlines the major points of entry.

Austria From Innsbruck to Bolzano via A22/E45 (Brenner Pass); Villach to Tarvisio via A23/E55.

France From Nice to Ventimiglia via A10/E80; Modane to Turin (Torino) via A32/E70 (Fréjus Tunnel); Chamonix to Courmayeur via A5/E25 (Mont Blanc Tunnel).

Slovenia From Sežana to Trieste via SS58/E70.

Switzerland From Martigny to Aosta via SS27/E27 (Grand St Bernard Tunnel); Lugano to Como via A9/E35.

SEA

International car ferries sail to Italy from Albania, Croatia, Greece, Malta, Montenegro, Morocco, Slovenia, Spain and Tunisia. Some routes only operate in summer, when ticket prices rise. Prices for vehicles vary according to their size. Car hire is not always available at ports, so check beforehand on the nearest agency.

The website www.traghettionline.com (in Italian) details all of the ferry companies in the Mediterranean. The principal operators serving Italy:

Agoudimos Lines (www.agoudimos.it) Greece to Bari (11 to 16 hours) and Brindisi (seven to 14 hours).

Endeavor Lines (www.endeavor-lines.com) Greece to Brindisi (seven to 14 hours).

Grandi Navi Veloci (www.gnv.it) Barcelona to Genoa (18 hours).

Jadrolinija (www.jadrolinija.hr) Croatia to Ancona (from nine hours) and Bari (10 hours).

Minoan Lines (www.minoan.gr) Greece to Venice (22 to 30 hours) and Ancona (16 to 22 hours).

Montenegro Lines (www.montenegrolines. net) Bar to Bari (nine hours).

Superfast (www.superfast.com) Greece to Bari (11 to 16 hours) and Ancona (16 to 22 hours).

Ventouris (www.ventouris.gr) Albania to Bari (eight hours).

TRAIN

Regular trains on two western lines connect Italy with France (one along the coast and the other from Turin into the French Alps). Trains from Milan head north into Switzerland and on towards the Benelux countries. Further east, two lines connect with Central and Eastern Europe.

Trenitalia (www.trenitalia.com) offers various train and car-hire packages that allow you to save on hire charges when you book a train ticket – see the website for details.

DIRECTORY A–Z

ACCOMMODATION

From dreamy villas to chic boutique hotels, historic hideaways and ravishing farmstays, Italy offers accommodation to suit every taste and budget.

Seasons & Rates

➡ Hotel rates fluctuate enormously from high to low season, and even from day to day

depending on demand, season and booking method (online, through an agency etc).

➡ As a rule, peak rates apply at Easter, in summer and over the Christmas/New Year period. But there are exceptions – in the mountains, high season means the ski season (December to late March). Also, August is high season on the coast but low season in many cities where hotels offer discounts.

➡ Southern Italy is generally cheaper than the north.

Reservations

➡ Always book ahead in peak season, even if it's only for the first night or two.

➡ In the off-season, it always pays to call ahead to check that your hotel is open. Many coastal hotels close for winter, typically opening from late March to late October.

➡ Hotels usually require that reservations be confirmed with a credit-card number. No-shows will be docked a night's accommodation.

B&Bs

B&Bs can be found throughout the country in both urban and rural settings. Options include restored farmhouses, city *palazzi* (mansions), seaside bungalows and rooms in family houses. Prices vary but as a rule B&Bs are often better value than hotels in the same category. Note that breakfast in an Italian B&B will often be a continental combination of bread rolls, croissants, ham and cheese. For more information, contact **Bed & Breakfast Italia** (www.bbitalia.it).

Hotels & Pensioni

A *pensione* is a small, family-run hotel or guesthouse. Hotels are bigger and more expensive than *pensioni*, although at the cheaper end of the market, there's often little difference between the two. All hotels are rated from one to five stars, although this rating relates to facilities only and

Sleeping Price Ranges

The price ranges listed in this book refer to a double room with bathroom.

€ less than €100

€€ €100–200

€€€ more than €200

gives no indication of value, comfort, atmosphere or friendliness.

Breakfast in cheaper hotels is rarely worth setting the alarm for. If you have the option, save your money and pop into a bar for a coffee and *cornetto* (croissant).

➡ One-star hotels and *pensioni* tend to be basic and often do not offer private bathrooms.

➡ Two-star places are similar but rooms will generally have a private bathroom.

➡ Three-star hotel rooms will come with a hairdryer, minibar (or fridge), safe and air-con. Many will also have satellite TV and wi-fi.

➡ Four- and five-star hotels offer facilities such as room service, laundry and dry-cleaning.

Agriturismi

From rustic country houses to luxurious estates and fully functioning farms, Italian farmstays, known as *agriturismi* (singular – *agriturismo*) are hugely popular. Comfort levels, facilities and prices vary accordingly but the best will offer swimming pools and top-class accommodation. Many also operate restaurants specialising in traditional local cuisine.

Agriturismi have long thrived in Tuscany and Umbria, but you'll now find them across the country. For listings and further details, check out the following sites:

Agriturismo.com (www.agriturismo.com)

Agriturismo.it (www.agriturismo.it)

Agriturismo-Italia.net (www.agriturismo-italia.net)

Agriturismo.net (www.agriturismo.net)

Agriturismo Vero (www.agriturismo vero.com)

Agriturist (www.agriturist.com)

Other Options

Camping A popular summer option. Most campsites are big, summer-only complexes with swimming pools, restaurants and supermarkets. Many have space for RVs and offer bungalows or simple, self-contained flats. Minimum stays sometimes apply in high season. Check out www.campeggi.com and www.camping.it.

Hostels Hostels around the country offer dorm beds and private rooms. Breakfast is usually included in rates and dinner is sometimes available for about €10. For listings and further details, see www.aighostels.com or www.hostelworld.com.

Book Your Stay Online

For more accommodation reviews by Lonely Planet authors, check out lonelyplanet.com/italy/hotels. You'll find independent reviews, as well as recommendations on the best places to stay. Best of all, you can book online.

Convents & Monasteries Some convents and monasteries provide basic accommodation. Expect curfews, few frills and value for money. Useful resources include www.monasterystays.com, www.initaly.com/agri/convents.htm and www.santasusanna.org/comingToRome/convents.html.

Refuges Mountain huts kitted out with bunk rooms sleeping anything from two to a dozen or more people. Many offer half-board (bed, breakfast and dinner) and most are open from mid-June to mid-September.

Villas Villas and *fattorie* (farmhouses) can be rented in their entirety or sometimes by the room. Many have swimming pools.

ELECTRICITY

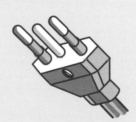

230V/50Hz

120V/60Hz

FOOD

A full Italian meal consists of an antipasto (appetiser), *primo* (first course, usually a pasta, risotto or polenta), *secondo* (second course, meat or fish) with *contorno* (vegetable side dish) or *insalata* (salad), and *dolce* (dessert) and/or fruit. When eating out it's perfectly OK to mix and match and order, say, a *primo* followed by an *insalata* or *contorno*.

Where to Eat

Trattorias Traditional, often family-run eateries offering simple, local food and wine. Some newer-wave trattorias offer more creative fare and scholarly wine lists. Generally cheap to midrange in price.

Eating Price Ranges

The following price ranges refer to a meal consisting of a *primo* (first course), *secondo* (second course), *dolce* (dessert) and a glass of house wine for one:

€ less than €25

€€ €25–45

€€€ more than €45

Restaurants More formal, and more expensive, than trattorias, with more choice and smarter service. Reservations are generally required for popular and top-end places.

Pizzerias Alongside pizza, many pizzerias also offer antipasti, pastas, meat and vegetable dishes. They're often only open in the evening. The best have a wood-oven (*forno a legna*).

Bars & Cafes Italians often breakfast on *cornetti* and coffee at a bar or cafe. Many bars and cafes sell *panini* (bread rolls with simple fillings) at lunchtime and serve a hot and cold buffet during the early evening *aperitivo* (aperitif) hour.

Wine Bars At an *enoteca* (plural – *enoteche*) you can drink wine by the glass and eat snacks such as cheeses, cold meats, bruschette and *crostini* (little toasts). Some also serve hot dishes.

Markets Most towns and cities have morning produce markets where you can stock up on picnic provisions. Villages might have a weekly market.

GAY & LESBIAN TRAVELLERS

➡ Homosexuality is legal in Italy and well tolerated in the major cities. However, overt displays of affection by homosexual couples could attract a negative response, particularly in the more conservative south and in smaller towns.

➡ There are gay clubs in Rome, Milan and Bologna, and a handful in places such as Florence (Firenze). Some coastal towns and resorts (such as Viareggio in Tuscany and Taormina in Sicily) see much more action in summer.

Useful resources:

Arcigay & Arcilesbica (www.arcigay.it) Bologna-based national organisation for gays and lesbians.

GayFriendlyItaly.com (www.gayfriendly italy.com) English-language site produced by Gay.it, with information on everything from hotels to homophobia issues and the law.

Gay.it (www.gay.it) Website listing gay bars and hotels across the country.

Pride (www.prideonline.it) National monthly magazine of art, music, politics and gay culture.

HEALTH

➡ Italy has a public health system that is legally bound to provide emergency care to everyone.

➡ EU nationals are entitled to reduced-cost, sometimes free, medical care with a European Health Insurance Card (EHIC), available from your home health authority.

➡ Non-EU citizens should take out medical insurance.

➡ For emergency treatment, you can go to the *pronto soccorso* (casualty) section of an *ospedale* (public hospital), though be prepared for a long wait.

➡ Pharmacists can give advice and sell over-the-counter medication for minor illnesses. Pharmacies generally keep the same hours as other shops, closing at night and on Sundays. A handful remain open on a rotation basis *(farmacie di turno)* for emergency purposes. These are usually listed in newspapers. Closed pharmacies display a list of the nearest ones open.

➡ In major cities you are likely to find English-speaking doctors or a translator service available.

➡ Italian tap water is fine to drink.

➡ No vaccinations are required for travel to Italy.

INTERNET ACCESS

➡ An increasing number of hotels, B&Bs, hostels and even *agriturismi* offer free wi-fi. You'll also find it in many bars and cafes.

➡ The 🛜 icon used throughout this book indicates wi-fi is available.

➡ Rome and Bologna are among the cities that provide free wi-fi, although you'll have to register for the service at www.romawireless.com (Rome) and www.comune.bologna.it/wireless (Bologna) and have an Italian mobile phone number.

➡ Venice (Venezia) offers pay-for wi-fi packages online at www.veniceconnected.com.

➡ Internet access is not as widespread in rural and southern Italy as in urban and northern areas.

➡ Internet cafes are thin on the ground. Typical charges range from €2 to €6 per hour. They might require formal photo ID.

➡ Many top-end hotels charge upwards of €10 per day for access.

Italian Wine Classifications

Italian wines are classified according to strict quality-control standards and carry one of four denominations:

DOCG (Denominazione di Origine Controllata e Garantita) Italy's best wines; made in specific areas according to stringent production rules.

DOC (Denominazione di Origine Controllata) Quality wines produced in defined regional areas.

IGT (Indicazione geografica tipica) Wines typical of a certain region.

VdT (Vino da Tavola) Wines for everyday drinking; often served as house wine in trattorias.

MONEY

Italy uses the euro. Euro notes come in denominations of €500, €200, €100, €50, €20, €10 and €5; coins come in denominations of €2 and €1, and 50, 20, 10, five, two and one cents.

For the latest exchange rates, check out www.xe.com.

Admission Prices

➡ There are no hard and fast rules, but many state museums and galleries offer discounted admission to EU seniors and students.

➡ Typically, EU citizens under 18 and over 65 enter free and those aged between 18 and 24 pay a reduced rate.

➡ EU teachers might also qualify for concessions. In all cases you'll need photo ID to claim reduced entry.

ATMs

ATMs (known as *bancomat*) are widely available throughout Italy and are the best way to obtain local currency.

Credit Cards

➡ International credit and debit cards can be used in any ATM displaying the appropriate sign. Visa and MasterCard are among the most widely recognised, but others such as Cirrus and Maestro are also well covered.

Tipping Guide

Taxis Round the fare up to the nearest euro.

Restaurants Many locals don't tip waiters, but most visitors leave 10% if there's no service charge.

Cafes Leave a coin (as little as €0.10 is acceptable) if you drank your coffee at the counter, or 10% if you sat at a table.

Hotels Bellhops usually expect €1 to €2 per bag; it's not necessary to tip the concierge, cleaners or front-desk staff.

➡ Only some banks give cash advances over the counter, so you're better off using ATMs.

➡ Cards are good for paying in most hotels, restaurants, shops, supermarkets and toll booths. Some cheaper *pensioni*, trattorias and pizzerias only accept cash. Don't rely on credit cards at museums or galleries.

➡ Check any charges with your bank. Most banks now build a fee of around 2.75% into every foreign transaction. Also, ATM withdrawals can attract a further fee, usually around 1.5%.

➡ In an emergency, call to have your card blocked:

Amex (☑06 7290 0347 or your national call number)

Diners Club (☑800 393939)

MasterCard (☑800 870866)

Visa (☑800 819014)

Moneychangers

You can change money in banks, at post offices or at a *cambio* (exchange office). Post offices and banks tend to offer the best rates; exchange offices keep longer hours, but watch for high commissions and inferior rates.

OPENING HOURS

Banks 8.30am to 1.30pm and 2.45pm to 4.30pm Monday to Friday.

Bars & Cafes 7.30am to 8pm, sometimes until 1am or 2am.

Clubs 10pm to 4am.

Post Offices Main offices 8am to 7pm Monday to Friday, 8.30am to noon Saturday; branches 8am to 2pm weekdays, 8.30am to noon Saturday.

Restaurants Noon to 3pm and 7.30pm to 11pm; sometimes later in summer and in the south. Kitchens often shut an hour earlier than final closing time; most places close at least one day a week.

Shops 9am to 1pm and 3.30pm to 7.30pm (or 4pm to 8pm) weekdays. In larger cities, department stores and supermarkets typically open 9am to 7.30pm or 10am to 8pm Monday to Saturday, some also on Sunday.

PUBLIC HOLIDAYS

Individual towns have public holidays to celebrate the feasts of their patron saints. National public holidays:

Capodanno (New Year's Day) 1 January

Epifania (Epiphany) 6 January

Pasquetta (Easter Monday) March/April

Giorno della Liberazione (Liberation Day) 25 April

Festa del Lavoro (Labour Day) 1 May

Festa della Repubblica (Republic Day) 2 June

Festa dei Santi Pietro e Paolo (Feast of St Peter & St Paul) 29 June

Ferragosto (Feast of the Assumption) 15 August

Festa di Ognisanti (All Saints' Day) 1 November

Festa dell'Immacolata Concezione (Feast of the Immaculate Conception) 8 December

Natale (Christmas Day) 25 December

Festa di Santo Stefano (Boxing Day) 26 December

SAFE TRAVEL

Italy is a safe country but petty theft can be a problem. There's no need for paranoia but be aware that thieves and pickpockets operate in touristy areas, so watch out when exploring the sights in Rome, Florence, Venice, Naples (Napoli) etc.

Cars, particularly those with foreign number plates or rental-company stickers, provide rich pickings for thieves – see p120.

In case of theft or loss, report the incident to the police within 24 hours and ask for a statement. Some tips:

➡ Keep essentials in a money belt but carry your day's spending money in a separate wallet.

➡ Wear your bag/camera strap across your body and away from the road – thieves on mopeds can swipe a bag and be gone in seconds.

➡ Never drape your bag over an empty chair at a street-side cafe or put it where you can't see it.

➡ Always check your change to see you haven't been short changed.

TELEPHONE

Domestic Calls

➡ Italian telephone area codes all begin with 0 and consist of up to four digits. Area codes are an integral part of all Italian phone numbers and must be dialled even when calling locally.

➡ Mobile-phone numbers are nine or 10 digits and have a three-digit prefix starting with a 3.

➡ Toll-free (free-phone) numbers are known as *numeri verdi* and usually start with 800.

➡ Non-geographical numbers start with 840, 841, 848, 892, 899, 163, 166 or 199. Some six-digit national rate numbers are also in use (such as those for Alitalia, rail and postal information).

International Calls

➡ To call Italy from abroad, call the international access number (☎011 in the USA, ☎00 from most other countries), Italy's country code (☎39) and then the area code of the location you want, including the leading 0.

➡ The cheapest options for calling internationally are free or low-cost computer programs such as Skype, cut-rate call centres and international calling cards.

➡ Cut-price call centres can be found in all of the main cities, and rates can be considerably lower than from Telecom payphones.

➡ Another alternative is to use a direct-dialling service such as AT&T's USA Direct (access number ☎800 172444) or Telstra's Australia Direct (access number ☎800 172610), which allows you to make a reverse-charge (collect) call at home-country rates.

➡ To make a reverse-charge international call from a public telephone, dial ☎170.

Mobile Phones (Cell Phones)

➡ Italy uses GSM 900/1800, which is compatible with the rest of Europe and Australia but not with North American GSM 1900 or the totally different Japanese system.

➡ Most smart phones are multiband, meaning that they are compatible with a variety of international networks. Check with your service provider to make sure it is compatible and beware of calls being routed internationally (very expensive for a 'local' call). In many cases you're better off buying an Italian phone or unlocking your phone for use with an Italian SIM card.

➡ If you have a GSM multiband phone that you can unlock, it can cost as little as €10 to activate a prepaid SIM card in Italy. **TIM** (Telecom Italia Mobile; www.tim.it), **Wind** (www.wind.it) and **Vodafone** (www.vodafone.it) offer SIM cards and have retail outlets across Italy. You'll usually need your passport to open an account.

➡ Once you're set up with a SIM card, you can easily purchase recharge cards (allowing you to top up your account with extra minutes) at tobacconists and news stands, as well as some bars, supermarkets and banks.

Payphones & Phonecards

➡ You'll find payphones on the streets, in train stations and in Telecom offices. Most accept only *carte/schede telefoniche* (phonecards), although some accept credit cards.

Important Numbers

Italy country code (☎39)

International access code (☎00)

Police (☎113)

Carabinieri (military police; ☎112)

Ambulance (☎118)

Fire (☎115)

Roadside assistance (☎803 116 from a landline or mobile with an Italian provider; ☎800 116800 from a foreign mobile phone)

➡ Telecom offers a range of prepaid cards; for a full list, see www.telecomitalia.it/telefono/carte-telefoniche.

➡ You can buy phonecards at post offices, tobacconists and news stands.

TOILETS

➡ Public toilets are thin on the ground in Italy. You'll find them in autostrada service stations (generally free) and in main train stations (usually with a small fee of between €0.50 and €1).

➡ Often, the best thing is to nip into a cafe or bar, although you'll probably have to order a quick drink first.

➡ Keep some tissues to hand as loo paper is rare.

TOURIST INFORMATION

Practically every village, town and city in Italy has a tourist office of sorts. These operate under a variety of names: Azienda di Promozione Turistica (APT), Azienda Autonoma di Soggiorno e Turismo (AAST), Informazione e Assistenza ai Turisti (IAT) and Pro Loco. All deal directly with the public and most will respond to written and telephone requests for information.

Tourist offices can usually provide a city map, lists of hotels and information on the major sights. In larger towns and major tourist areas, English is usually spoken.

Main offices are generally open Monday to Friday; some also open on weekends, especially in urban areas and in peak summer season. Info booths (at train stations, for example) may keep slightly different hours.

Tourist Authorities
The **Italian National Tourist Office** (ENIT; www.enit.it) maintains international offices. See the website for contact details.

Regional tourist authorities are more concerned with planning, marketing and promotion than with offering a public information service. However, they offer useful websites such as:

Campania (www.in-campania.com)

Other useful websites include www.italia.it and www.easy-italia.com.

TRAVELLERS WITH DISABILITIES

Italy is not an easy country for travellers with disabilities. Cobbled streets, blocked pavements and tiny lifts cause problems for wheelchair users. Not a lot has been done to make life easier for the deaf or blind, either.

A handful of cities publish general guides on accessibility, among them Bologna, Milan, Padua (Padova), Reggio Emilia, Turin, Venice and Verona. Contact the relevant tourist authorities for further information. Other helpful resources:

Handy Turismo (www.handyturismo.it) Information on Rome.

Milano per Tutti (www.milanopertutti.it) Covers Milan.

Lonely Planet (lptravel.to/AccessibleTravel) A free accessible travel guide that can be downloaded from the website.

Useful organisations:

Accessible Italy (www.accessibleitaly.com) Specialises in holiday services for travellers with disabilities. This is the best first port of call.

Consorzio Cooperative Integrate (www.coinsociale.it) This Rome-based organisation provides information on the capital (including transport and access) and is happy to share its contacts throughout Italy. Its **Presidio del Lazio** (www.presidiolazio.it) program seeks to improve access for tourists with disabilities.

Tourism for All (www.tourismforall.org.uk) This UK-based group has information on hotels with access for guests with disabilities, where to hire equipment and tour operators dealing with travellers with disabilities.

VISAS

➡ EU citizens do not need a visa for Italy.

➡ Residents of 28 non-EU countries, including Australia, Brazil, Canada, Israel, Japan, New Zealand and the USA, do not require visas for tourist visits of up to 90 days.

➡ Italy is one of the 15 signatories of the Schengen Convention. The standard tourist visa for a Schengen country is valid for 90 days. You must apply for it in your country of residence and you cannot apply for more than two in any 12-month period. They are not renewable within Italy.

➡ For full details of Italy's visa requirements check www.esteri.it/visti/home_eng.asp.

Language

Italian sounds can all be found in English. If you read our coloured pronunciation guides as if they were English, you'll be understood. Note that ai is pronounced as in 'aisle', ay as in 'say', ow as in 'how', dz as the 'ds' in 'lids', and that r is strong and rolled. If the consonant is written as a double letter, it's pronounced a little stronger, eg *sonno son·*no (sleep) versus *sono so·*no (I am). The stressed syllables are indicated with italics.

BASICS

Hello.	*Buongiorno.*	bwon·*jor*·no
Goodbye.	*Arrivederci.*	a·ree·ve·*der*·chee
Yes./No.	*Sì./No.*	see/no
Excuse me.	*Mi scusi.*	mee *skoo*·zee
Sorry.	*Mi dispiace.*	mee dees·*pya*·che
Please.	*Per favore.*	per fa·*vo*·re
Thank you.	*Grazie.*	*gra*·tsye

You're welcome.
Prego.   *pre*·go

Do you speak English?
Parli inglese?   *par*·lee een·*gle*·ze

I don't understand.
Non capisco.   non ka·*pee*·sko

How much is this?
Quanto costa questo?   *kwan*·to *kos*·ta *kwe*·sto

ACCOMMODATION

Do you have a room?
Avete una camera?   a·*ve*·te oo·na *ka*·me·ra

How much is it per night/person?
*Quanto costa per   *kwan*·to *kos*·ta per
una notte/persona?*   oo·na *no*·te/per·*so*·na

DIRECTIONS

Where's ...?
Dov'è ...?   do·*ve* ...

Can you show me (on the map)?
*Può mostrarmi   pwo mos·*trar*·mee
(sulla pianta)?*   (soo·la *pyan*·ta)

EATING & DRINKING

What would you recommend?
Cosa mi consiglia?   *ko*·za mee kon·*see*·lya

I'd like ..., please.
Vorrei ..., per favore.   vo·*ray* ... per fa·*vo*·re

I don't eat (meat).
Non mangio (carne).   non *man*·jo (*kar*·ne)

Please bring the bill.
*Mi porta il conto,   mee *por*·ta eel *kon*·to
per favore?*   per fa·*vo*·re

EMERGENCIES

Help!
Aiuto!   a·*yoo*·to

I'm lost.
Mi sono perso/a. (m/f)   mee *so*·no per·so/a

I'm ill.
Mi sento male.   mee *sen*·to ma·le

Call the police!
Chiami la polizia!   *kya*·mee la po·lee·*tsee*·a

Call a doctor!
Chiami un medico!   *kya*·mee oon me·*dee*·ko

Want More?

For in-depth language information and handy phrases, check out Lonely Planet's *Italian Phrasebook*. You'll find it at **shop.lonelyplanet.com**.

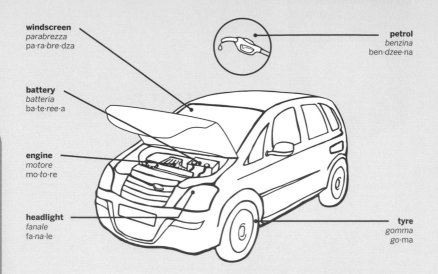

windscreen
parabrezza
pa·ra·bre·dza

petrol
benzina
ben·dzee·na

battery
batteria
ba·te·ree·a

engine
motore
mo·to·re

headlight
fanale
fa·na·le

tyre
gomma
go·ma

Signs

Alt	Stop
Dare la Precedenza	Give Way
Deviazione	Detour
Divieto di Accesso	No Entry
Entrata	Entrance
Pedaggio	Toll
Senso Unico	One Way
Uscita	Exit

ON THE ROAD

I'd like to hire a/an ...	*Vorrei noleggiare ...*	vo·ray no·le·ja·re ...
4WD	*un fuoristrada*	oon fwo·ree·stra·da
automatic/ manual	*una macchina automatica/ manuale*	oo·na ma·kee·na ow·to·ma·tee·ka/ ma·noo·a·le
motorbike	*una moto*	oo·na mo·to

How much is it ...?	*Quanto costa ...?*	kwan·to kos·ta ...
daily	*al giorno*	al jor·no
weekly	*alla settimana*	a·la se·tee·ma·na

Does that include insurance?
E' compresa l'assicurazione?
e kom·pre·sa la·see·koo·ra·tsyo·ne

Does that include mileage?
E' compreso il chilometraggio?
e kom·pre·so eel kee·lo·me·tra·jo

What's the city/country speed limit?
Qual'è il limite di velocità in città/campagna?
kwa·le eel lee·mee·te dee ve·lo·chee·ta een chee·ta/kam·pa·nya

Is this the road to (Venice)?
Questa strada porta a (Venezia)?
kwe·sta stra·da por·ta a (ve·ne·tsya)

(How long) Can I park here?
(Per quanto tempo) Posso parcheggiare qui?
(per kwan·to tem·po) po·so par·ke·ja·re kwee

Where's a service station?
Dov'è una stazione di servizio?
do·ve oo·na sta·tsyo·ne dee ser·vee·tsyo

Please fill it up.
Il pieno, per favore.
eel pye·no per fa·vo·re

I'd like (30) litres.
Vorrei (trenta) litri.
vo·ray (tren·ta) lee·tree

Please check the oil/water.
Può controllare l'olio/ l'acqua, per favore?
pwo kon·tro·la·re lo·lyo/ la·kwa per fa·vo·re

I need a mechanic.
Ho bisogno di un meccanico.
o bee·zo·nyo dee oon me·ka·nee·ko

The car/motorbike has broken down.
La macchina/moto si è guastata.
la ma·kee·na/mo·to see e gwas·ta·ta

I had an accident.
Ho avuto un incidente.
o a·voo·to oon een·chee·den·te

BEHIND THE SCENES

SEND US YOUR FEEDBACK

We love to hear from travellers – your comments help make our books better. We read every word, and we guarantee that your feedback goes straight to the authors. Visit **lonelyplanet. com/contact** to submit your updates and suggestions.

Note: We may edit, reproduce and incorporate your comments in Lonely Planet products such as guidebooks, websites and digital products, so let us know if you don't want your comments reproduced or your name acknowledged. For a copy of our privacy policy visit lonelyplanet.com/privacy.

ACKNOWLEDGMENTS

Climate map data adapted from Peel MC, Finlayson BL & McMahon TA (2007) 'Updated World Map of the Köppen-Geiger Climate Classification', *Hydrology and Earth System Sciences*, 11, 163344.

Illustration pp68–9 by Javier Martinez Zarracina.

Cover photographs: Front: The road from Amalfi to Atrani, Mark Avellino/ Getty Images; Back: Statue of Pan, Positano, Buena Vista Images/Getty Images

THIS BOOK

This 1st edition of Lonely Planet's *Amalfi Coast Road Trips* guidebook was researched and written by Cristian Bonetto, Duncan Garwood, Paula Hardy, Robert Landon and Helena Smith. This guidebook was produced by the following:

Destination Editor Anna Tyler

Product Editor Grace Dobell

Senior Cartographers Valentina Kremenchutskaya, Anthony Phelan

Book Designer Wendy Wright

Assisting Editor Bruce Evans

Cover Researcher Naomi Parker

Thanks to Shahara Ahmed, Joel Cotterell, Brendan Dempsey, Darren O'Connell, Kirsten Rawlings, Alison Ridgway, Victoria Smith, Angela Tinson, Tony Wheeler

OUR STORY

A beat-up old car, a few dollars in the pocket and a sense of adventure. In 1972 that's all Tony and Maureen Wheeler needed for the trip of a lifetime – across Europe and Asia overland to Australia. It took several months, and at the end – broke but inspired – they sat at their kitchen table writing and stapling together their first travel guide, *Across Asia on the Cheap*. Within a week they'd sold 1500 copies. Lonely Planet was born.

Today, Lonely Planet has offices in Franklin, London, Melbourne, Oakland, Beijing and Delhi, with more than 600 staff and writers. We share Tony's belief that 'a great guidebook should do three things: inform, educate and amuse'.

INDEX

ROBERT LANDON

Ten minutes into his maiden voyage to Italy, Robert was pickpocketed in a Florence church, yet he has been returning obsessively ever since, including stints living in Rome and Florence. He has authored Lonely Planet guides to *Florence*, *Venice* and *Brazil*, and has also written about travel, art and architecture for the *Los Angeles Times*, *Dwell*, *Metropolis* and many other publications.

Read more about Robert at: auth.lonelyplanet. com/profiles/robertlandon

HELENA SMITH

Helena Smith has been visiting Italy since she was five years old. At that time chocolate spread on toast was the main draw – now she goes back for the food, the warmth, the art and the atmosphere. Researching this edition took her from mountain walks with sea views to the stunning Greek temples of Paestum.

OUR WRITERS

CRISTIAN BONETTO

Despite being the son of northern Italians, Cristian has an enduring weakness for Naples and Campania. It took one visit as a young backpacker to get him hooked, and the Australian-born writer has been covering the region's food, culture and lifestyle for more than a decade. According to Cristian, no Italian city quite matches Naples' complexity and intrigue, and its ability to constantly surprise and contradict makes it a thrill to write about. The writer's musings have appeared in publications across the globe, and his Naples-based play *Il Cortile* (The Courtyard) has toured numerous Italian cities. Cristian has contributed to more than 30 Lonely Planet guides, including *Venice & the Veneto*, *New York City*, *Denmark* and *Singapore*. You can follow Cristian's adventures on Twitter (@CristianBonetto) and on Instagram (@rexcat75).

DUNCAN GARWOOD

Ever since moving to Italy in 1997, Duncan has spent much of his time driving the country on assignment for Lonely Planet. He's clocked up tens of thousands of kilometres and contributed to a whole host of Lonely Planet guidebooks, including *Italy*, *Rome*, *Sicily*, *Sardinia* and *Naples*, as well as the *Food Lover's Guide to the World*. He currently lives in the Castelli Romani hills just outside of Rome.

Read more about Duncan at: auth.lonelyplanet. com/profiles/duncangarwood

PAULA HARDY

Paula's first experience of northern Italy was Furniture Fair madness in Milan, braving frigid lake waters out of season and a suitcase full of impractical shoes. Now with over a decade of experience in contributing to Lonely Planet's Italy books, including five editions of *Italy*, *Pocket Milan*, *Puglia & Basilicata*, *Sicily* and *Sardinia*, she knows better and now shops in sensible shoes to work off the worst excesses of the Italian table. You can find her tweeting from the lakes and mountains @paula6hardy.

 MORE WRITERS

Published by Lonely Planet Publications Pty Ltd
ABN 36 005 607 983
1st edition – Jun 2016
ISBN 978 1 76034 055 1
© Lonely Planet 2016   Photographs © as indicated 2016
10 9 8 7 6 5 4 3 2 1
Printed in China

Although the authors and Lonely Planet have taken all reasonable care in preparing this book, we make no warranty about the accuracy or completeness of its content and, to the maximum extent permitted, disclaim all liability arising from its use.